Collins
Chinese
Language
— *and* —
Culture

HarperCollins Publishers
Westerhill Road
Bishopbriggs
Glasgow
G64 2QT
Great Britain

First Edition 2012

ISBN 978-0-00-745910-0

Reprint 10 9 8 7 6 5 4 3 2 1 0

©HarperCollins Publishers 2012

Collins® is a registered trademark of
HarperCollins Publishers Limited

www.collinslanguage.com

A catalogue record for this book is
available from the British Library

Typeset by Davidson Publishing Solutions,
Glasgow

Printed in Great Britain by Clays Ltd,
St Ives plc

Acknowledgements
We would like to thank those authors and
publishers who kindly gave permission for
copyright material to be used in the Collins
Word Web. We would also like to thank
Times Newspapers Ltd for providing
valuable data.

WRITTEN BY
Duncan Poupard

ILLUSTRATIONS BY
Li Na

EDITORS
Lisa Sutherland
Morven Dooner

FOR THE PUBLISHER
Freddy Chick
Lucy Cooper
Elaine Higgleton
Susanne Reichert

Contents

List of illustrations

Foreword

As China's influence on world affairs continues to grow in the twenty-first century, people are becoming increasingly curious about this historic country and its ways of life. This book is designed as a primer to engage that curiosity and dispel some of the myths that have grown up around China and its language.

This book aims to introduce aspects of Chinese life and culture to the English-speaking reader, while at the same time presenting interesting features of the Chinese language. It makes no claims at being comprehensive, for that would be an almost impossible task considering China's history and size. The book does not serve to bridge East and West, nor does it mean to. It is merely a taster, and hopefully the various jottings and anecdotes contained within will capture the reader's interest.

Chinese characters and their pinyin Romanizations are provided where possible to assist the student of Chinese. Proverbs and popular sayings in Chinese occur throughout the book, in places where they may help the reader to gain a fuller understanding of the context. Several 'how-to' and language guides are also included within the text, and it is hoped these may be of some small use to those travelling or living in China.

A book of this scope is bound to contain inaccuracies and oversights. All errors, omissions, or other defects are the sole responsibility of the author.

Chapter 1:
Introduction
序
xù

Introduction

序
xù

> *Even when one does not live in China one sometimes thinks of her as an old, great, big country which remains aloof from the world and does not quite belong to it.*
>
> **Lin Yutang**

China, for so long the symbol of the 'unfathomable' East, is no longer as mysterious as it once was. People from all over the world now travel, do business, or live in China. As China slowly emerges as a superpower, it increasingly finds itself the focus of Western news reports, books, and other media.

Yet despite this flurry of interest, China's language and culture still form a barrier to inter-cultural understanding. Its written language is almost impossible to grasp without years of study, and its spoken language is marked by a diversity of dialects that seem for all the world like different languages. Even if the language barrier is overcome, China's culture offers up an embarrassment of riches to the interested observer, many of its traditions dating back thousands of years. China is the oldest living nation with a continuous culture, and it is also the most populous country in the world. Once one of the world's largest empires, China also gave us some of mankind's greatest inventions, such as gunpowder and the compass, before falling far behind the pace in the latter half of the last millennium.

China is a country that defies categorization, and often explanation. Its sheer size means that what holds true in one corner of the country is often the exact opposite of the case in another. Hainan province in the south lies within the tropical belt, while Heilongjiang in the north is subarctic, with temperatures that reach 40 degrees below zero in winter. Only a powerful bureaucracy and a common culture prevented the country from breaking up into separate nations throughout its several thousand years of history.

The land

Considering its immense size, China has been fairly well isolated by its geographical barriers, which may have led to its relatively insular nature. To the east lies the Pacific Ocean, while steep gorges run along the Burmese border to the southwest, and the towering Tibetan plateau rises up as if to block the western border. The dry, sparse lands of Central Asia and Mongolia lie to the north. There is little doubt that these geographical factors helped China to develop her own distinctive culture, with very little foreign interference.

A tale of two rivers

China slopes down from west to east, from the high peaks of Tibet down to the shores of the Pacific Ocean, into which all its major rivers flow. The Yellow River, *Huánghé* 黄河, perhaps the ultimate symbol of Chinese civilization, is 2,700 miles in length, flowing east from the Tibetan plateau, looping around the Ordos desert, before finally flowing out into the Bohai Sea between the provinces of Liaoning and Shandong.

The Yellow River is so named for its perennially muddy colour. The Chinese have a folk saying, *Huánghé dǒu shuǐ, ní jū qī qī* 黄河斗水，泥居其七, which means 'a dipperful of Yellow River is seven tenths mud'. The river was historically liable to severe flooding. According to legend, one of China's very first emperors, Yu the Great, was responsible for taming the floods by building irrigation canals and dredging the riverbeds. In 1988, a controversial Chinese documentary, the *River Elegy* (*Héshāng* 河殇), contrasted China's 'yellow', river-based culture with the 'blue', ocean-going culture of the West. The programme attributed China's backwardness in the modern age to its failure to develop an exploratory seafaring culture.

At 3,200 miles in length, the Yangtze is China's longest river, and the sixth longest in the world. In Chinese, the Yangtze is known as the *Chángjiāng* 长江, the 'long river'. Only in its lower reaches past Yangzhou in Jiangsu is it known in China as the *Yángzǐ jiāng* 扬子江, the Yangtze. However, as this was the first name for the river that early Christian missionaries heard, it stuck. Cruise ships weighing 10,000 tonnes can voyage inland as far as Nanjing.

The Yangtze serves as the de facto dividing line between north and south, cutting the country in two. In the past, those areas south of the river were known as *jiāngnán* 江南, literally 'south of the river', while parts of the country north of the Yangtze were called *jiāngběi* 江北, 'north of the river'. In modern times *jiāngnán* has come to refer to a relatively small area encompassing Southern Jiangsu and Anhui provinces, as well as parts of Northern Zhejiang. This region is known for its scenic water towns and traditional architecture.

China administers 22 provinces, four municipalities (the capital, Beijing, and the metropolitan conurbations of Shanghai, Tianjin, and Chongqing), five autonomous regions and two special administrative regions (Hong Kong and Macau). Generally speaking, the eastern provinces are more heavily industrialized and developed, and therefore richer, than the western provinces, which rely more on agricultural production.

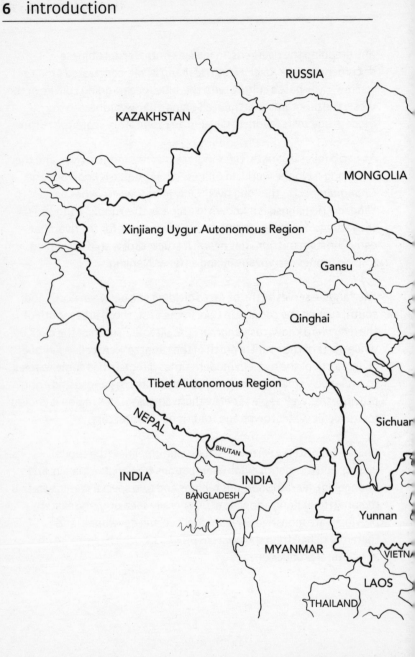

Map of modern China

The people

Despite continued migration into the cities, the majority of China's population is still rural, living in villages and small towns. China controls the movement of its population with the household register system, known as *hùkǒu* 户口. Every Chinese citizen has a *hùkǒu* which classifies them broadly as either an urban or a rural worker. It can be difficult for those with rural *hùkǒu* to make the transition into non-agricultural work in the cities. There is also a 'one child policy' in place to limit population growth. China is already the most populous country on earth, with over 1.3 billion people. In urban areas, families are permitted only one child, whereas in certain situations two children are permitted in the remote countryside.

People engaged in agricultural production are known as *nóngmín* 农民, 'farmers', and the word can also be used as an insult, referring to uncivilized or uncouth behaviour. In the cities, people are generally defined by the type of work they do. Those engaged in factory work or other manual labour are labelled 'blue collar workers' (*lánlǐng* 蓝领), while people in professional jobs are 'white-collars' (*báilǐng* 白领). Those with very highly paid jobs, such as upper management, are 'gold-collar' workers (*jīnlǐng* 金领). People who are lucky or well-connected enough to work for the government are called *gànbù* 干部, 'cadres', borrowing the old Communist terminology.

China is officially composed of 56 ethnic groups: notably 55 ethnic minorities, and the Han Chinese. The Han make up by far the majority of China's population – about 92 per cent. After the Han, the four largest groups are the Manchus (*Mǎn* 满), the Mongolians (*Méng* 蒙), the Muslims (*Huí* 回), and the Tibetans (*Zàng* 藏). The relatively new term *Zhōnghuá mínzú* 中华民族, the 'Chinese race', is used to refer to all people of the Chinese culture, inclusive of every ethnic group. Han chauvinism, the view that Han culture is superior to that of the minority groups, does exist, and members of China's ethnic minorities are sometimes subjected to racial abuse by their Han compatriots.

This has been used as a justification for the racial violence in the autonomous regions of Xinjiang and Tibet. To promote unity and harmony (*héxié* 和谐) within its borders, the state has given minority groups certain special privileges, such as boosting the marks of ethnic minority pupils in the high school entrance examinations. This has led to resentment among some members of the Han population.

Chinese ethnic groups in traditional dress (from left to right):
Tibetan, Mongolian, and Han

The language

A wealth of different languages and dialects are spoken across China. Mandarin Chinese, also known as *pǔtōnghuà* 普通话, 'the common speech', is the official language of the People's Republic of China. The sounds of the language are based on the Beijing dialect, but the vocabulary is drawn from the group of Chinese dialects spoken across northern, central, and southwestern China, which are together also known as 'Mandarin Chinese'. Over 70 per cent of China's population speaks Mandarin, and it is the language used in classrooms across China. Chinese students take national *pǔtōnghuà* exams that are designed to test their spoken accent. People who speak non-standard Mandarin would find it nearly impossible to get work on China's central television stations. Those who work as presenters for state television represent the unofficial 'standard' of the language, much like the BBC presenters did for English in mid twentieth century Britain. The government encourages everyone to speak *pǔtōnghuà*, and most client-facing jobs require proficiency in standard Chinese. In non-Mandarin speaking regions, it is common to see such signs as *qǐng jiǎng pǔtōnghuà* 请讲普通话, 'please speak *putonghua*'.

The word 'Mandarin' is borrowed directly from the Portuguese language. It was first used as a name for the officials of the Chinese court – and the word 'mandarin' is still used in this way today. The court officials of imperial China all spoke *guānhuà* 官话, or 'official speech', a precursor of today's standard Mandarin.

Aside from the common tongue, almost every region has its own specific dialect, and many of these are mutually unintelligible. Some say there are around 108 dialects in the province of Fujian alone. In the south, local dialects are significantly different from standard Mandarin. Wu dialects (*Wú* 吴) are spoken in and around the Yangtze delta, including the Shanghai region. Just less than 10 per cent of China's population speaks Wu. Dialects aside, some of China's ethnic groups speaks their own distinct languages, like the Tibetans, Mongolians, and the Yi.

China's historic world view

In Chinese, China is known as 'Zhongguo' (*Zhōngguó* 中国), often translated as the 'Middle Kingdom'. The central axis of the character *zhōng* 中 points to its meaning: 'central'. The Chinese civilization developed from settlements dotted around the lower reaches of the Yellow River, later known as the central plains, *zhōngyuán* 中原. The traditional Chinese belief is that their country was the centre of the world, and that the focal point of the country, at the very centre of their world, was the emperor himself, the 'son of heaven' (*tiānzǐ* 天子). Because the emperor was thought to rule by heavenly mandate, his realm was known as *tiānxià* 天下, which means, 'all under heaven'. Technically speaking, the Chinese believed that their emperor ruled over all the nations of the world. Outlying tribes and tributary states lay on the outskirts of this world view, and all outsiders or foreign nations were described by the Chinese as 'barbarian' (*yí* 夷). Amazingly, this practice lasted right up until the nineteenth century, when China was forced to sign the Treaty of Tianjin during the Second Opium War (1856–1860). One of the main clauses of the treaty was that the Chinese would no longer use the character *yí*, 'barbarian', to refer to British officials in their official documentation.

Mythology

When talking about Chinese mythology, it's best to begin at the beginning: with the creation myth. The most well-known creation story is that of the mythological giant, Pan Gu 盘古. The story of Pan Gu was first recorded fairly late-on in China's history, in the Three Kingdoms period (220–280 AD). The legend that explains the beginning of the world is known as *Pán Gǔ kāi tiāndì* 盘古开天地, or 'Pan Gu splits heaven and earth'.

Before heaven and earth were separated, the universe was said to have been in a state of chaos, with everything mixed together in the shape of an enormous egg. The giant, Pan Gu, awakening after having slept inside the egg for 18,000 years, saw only darkness around him. Tired of this perpetual night, he decided to break open the egg. He succeeded, but only after great effort. Thus, heaven and earth were separated and took shape. The clear, lighter part formed the heavens (the 'yang' energy), and the muddy, heavier part formed the earth (the 'yin' energy). Pan Gu then collapsed and died from his exertions. Pan Gu's head and his four limbs became China's Five Sacred Mountains (*Wǔyuè* 五岳), his blood and tears turned into rivers and streams, his left eye rose up and became the sun, while his right eye became the moon, and the hair on his head formed into the trees and grass. All natural phenomena, including the changing of the seasons and the weather in the sky, are said to have originated from Pan Gu's body.

> **THE FIVE SACRED MOUNTAINS**
> According to Chinese tradition, there are Five Sacred Mountains, known as *Wǔyuè* 五岳. These are: Mount Tai (*Tàishān* 泰山) in Shandong, Mount Hua (*Huáshān* 华山) in Shaanxi, Mount Heng (*Héngshān* 衡山) in Hunan, another Mount Heng (*Héngshān* 恆山) in Shanxi, and Mount Song (*Sōngshān* 嵩山) in Henan.

Nowadays, people say *zìcóng Pán Gǔ kāi tiāndì* 自从盘古开天地, 'ever since Pan Gu split the heavens and the earth', as a way of saying 'ever since that happened', referring to a particular event or situation.

Nü Wa

After Pan Gu created the world, it was filled with mountains and rivers and all kinds of beasts, but there were no people. Nü Wa 女娲, a female deity, was distraught with loneliness, so she decided to make some company for herself. One day, she crouched down beside a pool and scooped up a handful of yellow earth, and moulded it into the image of a woman. As she set the woman down onto the ground, she sprang into life. Satisfied with her work, Nü Wa began making more people, both men and women. After some time, she grew tired and stopped, but the world was large, and still very empty. She told the men and women to form pairs, marry, and have children. Thus Nü Wa represents fertility and marriage. In the Han dynasty, Nü Wa was depicted with a woman's head on the body of a snake. Some believe that she is a reflection of the matriarchal society that existed in some parts of China in the distant past.

The Yellow Emperor

The Yellow Emperor

According to legend, the Yellow Emperor (*Huángdì* 黄帝) was the first ancestor of the Chinese race. He grew up by the banks of the Ji River, in modern-day Shaanxi province, and so took the surname Ji. The Yellow Emperor's clan was said to have moved east and founded the cultures of the central plains, the first cultures of Chinese civilization, which the people later named *Huáxià* 華夏, an old name for China. It was upon this foundation that China's first imperial dynasty, the *Xià* 夏, is said to have been born. The Ji clan, also descendants of the Yellow Emperor, went on to found the Zhou dynasty that followed on from the Xia and Shang.

The Chinese call themselves *Yán Huáng zǐsūn* 炎黄子孙, which literally means the 'descendants of the Fiery Emperor and the Yellow Emperor'. The Fiery Emperor was another legendary Han Chinese ruler.

> ### THE CHINESE LOVE AFFAIR WITH YELLOW
> The Chinese consider yellow to be the defining colour of their race. Since time immemorial, they have called themselves the 'yellow race' (*huángzhǒng* 黄种). The Yellow River (*Huáng hé* 黄河) is known to be the cradle of Chinese civilization, the Yellow Emperor (*Huángdì* 皇帝) is seen as the father of the Chinese race, and Nü Wa used yellow earth (*huángtǔ* 黄土) to create mankind.

A brief history of China

Whenever the opportunity arises, the Chinese like to point out the age and importance of their culture – and for good reason, given its impressive length. The popular phrase '5,000 years of history and 7,000 years of culture' (*wǔqiān nián de lìshǐ, qīqiān nián de wénhuà* 五千年的历史，七千年的文化) is often used to stress this point. China's history clearly is not that old: its written history dates back some 3,500 years, although there is archaeological evidence for the existence of human civilization as far back as the Neolithic era.

Prehistory to the Warring States period (1.7 million years BC – 221 BC)

The remnants of Yuanmou man (*Yuánmóurén* 元谋人), discovered in Yunnan province in the 1960s, are the earliest fossils of human ancestors to have been unearthed in China. They were initially dated as far back as 1.7 million years BC, although this has since been contested. The Hemudu site excavated in Zhejiang province dates to between 5000–4500 BC, and is the earliest example of rice cultivation in the country.

The first dynasty, the Xia (*Xià* 夏), was allegedly founded in 2070 BC by the legendary ruler Yu the Great. It is described in historical chronicles such as the Han dynasty *Records of the Grand Historian*, but its existence is to this day disputed. By the Shang dynasty (*Shāng* 商, 1600–1046 BC), advanced bronze-making techniques had been developed, people had begun to craft ironware, and a writing system, known as the oracle bone script, had formed. In the tombs of the Xia kings, hundreds of commoners, who may have been slaves, were buried alive with their rulers.

The Zhou dynasty (*Zhōu* 周) was China's longest, lasting from 1045 to 256 BC. It marked the beginnings of feudal society in China, and its influence reached north of the Yangtze. It was in this period that philosophers first gave voice to the 'mandate of heaven' (*tiānmìng* 天命), the notion that the emperor ruled by divine right, but that his dethronement proved that the mandate had been lost. The dynasty was divided into two eras: the Western Zhou and the Eastern Zhou. The latter was further split into two periods, the Spring and Autumn period, and the Warring States period.

The Qin dynasty (221–206 BC)

The king of the state of Qin (*Qín* 秦) defeated his rivals, bringing an end to the Warring States period and creating the first unified feudal empire under a centralized bureaucracy. He took the name *Shǐ Huángdì* 始皇帝, the 'First Emperor', and is known as Qin Shi Huang 秦始皇.

> **DID YOU KNOW?**
> The English word 'China' probably derives from the Chinese word 'Qin', as in Qin dynasty. 'Qin' in early Wade-Giles Romanization is written 'Ch'in'.

Qin Shi Huang standardized the written language, the system of weights and measurements, and the currency used in his empire. Despite the dynasty only lasting for 20 years, the imperial systems put in place during the Qin were used by successive emperors for another 2,000 years. To defend against barbarian invaders, a 5,000 kilometre long 'great wall' was created by connecting the old packed-earth fortifications built by the various Warring States. An army of terracotta warriors, tasked with defending Qin Shi Huang in the afterlife, were discovered near his tomb in 1974.

The Han dynasty (206 BC–220 AD) and the Silk Road

Founded by Liu Bang in 206 BC, the Han dynasty (*Hàn* 汉) witnessed great technological leaps in the areas of agriculture, handicrafts, and commerce. During this period, China's population reached 50 million, and its territory expanded westward as far as the rim of the Tarim Basin in the modern-day region of Xinjiang. This made it possible for Chinese silk to be transported relatively securely across central Asia from the Han capital of Chang'an to the Roman Empire, along the Silk Road (*sīchóu zhī lù* 丝绸之路). Buddhism entered China in the first century AD, and paper-making was invented in 105 AD by the government official, Cai Lun 蔡伦. China's ethnic majority, the Han, are named after this dynasty.

The Tang dynasty (618–907 AD)

The Tang (*Táng* 唐) is seen as one of China's greatest dynasties. Chinatowns around the world are known as *Tángrénjiē* 唐人街, literally 'Tang people street', as *Tángrén* 唐人, 'Tang people', is another word for 'ethnic Chinese'. Block printing was invented during the Tang, and this period is seen as a 'golden age' of literature and art. Poetry became an important part of social life, and Tang poetry (*Tángshī* 唐诗) is held by many to be the pinnacle of the poetic form. The Tang dynasty is notable for the reign of Empress Wu Zetian, the only woman ever to bear the title of Empress Regnant.

The Song, Yuan, Ming, and Qing dynasties (960–1911 AD)

Fifty years after the demise of the Tang, an imperial army re-unified China and established the Song dynasty (*Sòng* 宋, 960–1279 AD). Developments such as movable type printing during the Song made China one of the most technologically advanced countries in the world.

In 1271, Mongol leader Kublai Khan, grandson of Genghis Khan, established the Yuan dynasty (*Yuán* 元, 1271–1368 AD), the first non-Chinese imperial dynasty. During Kublai Khan's reign, the Venetian traveller Marco Polo made his famous journey to China, where he was received in the capital Dadu 大都 (present day Beijing).

The Ming dynasty (*Míng* 明, 1368–1644) was founded by a Han Chinese peasant and former Buddhist monk, Zhu Yuanzhang. Between 1405 and 1433, the Ming admiral and eunuch Zheng commanded maritime voyages to Southeast Asia, the Indian Ocean, the Persian Gulf and East Africa. China's population reached 100 million during Ming times.

DYNASTIC ERA NAMES

Emperors customarily assumed an 'era name' (*niánhào* 年號) that changed every few years. By Ming and Qing times, emperors only used one motto for their whole reign. Because of this, Ming and Qing emperors are recognized by their era names. For example, *Qiánlóng* 乾隆, literally 'heavenly abundance', was the era name of the Qing emperor with the personal name Aixin-Jueluo Hongli 愛新覺羅弘曆, and the posthumous temple name *Gāozōng* 高宗, or 'High Ancestor'. Today, he is mostly referred to as 'the Qianlong Emperor'.

Constant wars with the Mongols had weakened the Ming dynasty, and in 1644 the Manchus invaded China from the north, capturing Beijing and establishing the last imperial dynasty, the Qing dynasty (*Qīng* 清, 1644–1911). The Manchu rulers were intent on protecting themselves from internal rebellion as well as foreign aggression. They conquered Outer Mongolia (now the Mongolian People's Republic) in the late seventeenth century, and established control over Tibet in the eighteenth century.

CHINESE EMPERORS: INTERESTING FACTS

Zhao Tuo (240–137 BC), founder of the kingdom of Nanyue, was the longest-lived emperor. He lived to be 103 years old.

Emperor Shang of the Han dynasty was the shortest-lived emperor. He lived for less than a year. He was also the youngest emperor to ascend the throne, taking power when only 100 days old.

The Kangxi Emperor of the Qing Dynasty had the longest reign, ruling for 61 years.

Emperor Modi of Jin (died 1234 AD) had the shortest reign, ruling for less than one full day before being killed by the Mongols.

Emperor Wu of Jin (236–290 AD) had the most concubines. He had over 10,000 concubines living in his royal palace.

Emperor Huizong of Song (1082–1135 AD) had the most children. He had a grand total of 66 children: 34 daughters and 32 sons.

A series of incursions, wars, and the signing of one-sided treaties that granted concessions and privileges to the Western powers damaged the Qing beyond repair. In 1911, Sun Yat-sen, the first president of the Republic of China, led the Xinhai Revolution (*Xīnhài gémìng* 辛亥革命), bringing an end to over two millennia of feudal rule.

Birth of the People's Republic

For almost a decade, the cause of republican revolution stuttered and faded, but was re-ignited on 4 May 1919. A struggle between the nationalist Guomindang (*Guómíndǎng* 国民党) government and the Communist Party (*Gòngchǎndǎng* 共产党) began. Mao Zedong embarked upon his epic Long March in October 1934. After the anti-Japanese war, the Communists seized control of the capital, announcing the founding of the People's Republic of China on 1 October 1949. The defeated Guomindang nationalists fled to Taiwan.

Chapter 2:
Pinyin
拼音

Pinyin
拼音

Latinization is a good instrument with which to overcome illiteracy.
Mao Zedong

What is *pinyin*?

The Chinese script is different from European scripts in that it has no alphabet. Instead, it uses tens of thousands of individual characters, each corresponding to a syllable with a distinct meaning. The largest print dictionary in China contains over 80,000 characters! Suffice to say, memorizing characters is a hard ask for any student, especially when compared with the 26-letter alphabet used in English.

To write Chinese using English letters, it must be 'Romanized' – the sounds need to be converted into Latin script. Pinyin is the official system for Romanizing Mandarin Chinese, or *pǔtōnghuà*. It is a way of representing the sound of the language, and is the primary tool that helps learners to pronounce Chinese words. It's a way of making Chinese more easily accessible. In Chinese, '*pīnyīn*' literally means 'spelled sound'.

Pinyin also uses four different tone marks to represent the four tones of Mandarin Chinese (see chapter three). As an example, the character for book, 书, is written *shū* in pinyin.

Origins of Romanization

One of the major difficulties confronting the first Jesuit missionaries who arrived in China during the sixteenth century was the language barrier. As any student of the language will tell you, Chinese is a tough language to learn, mostly because the script is so complex. To overcome this, the missionaries tried to write down the sounds of Chinese using the Latin alphabet. They did not want to completely get rid of Chinese characters, they just wanted to make their studies of the language easier.

> **DID YOU KNOW?**
> The name Confucius is not pinyin, but in fact an example of early missionary Romanization. In pinyin, Confucius is spelled *Kǒngfūzǐ*: this translates as 'Master Kong'. The 'ius' in Confucius is a Latin male noun ending.

Pinyin is the culmination of various official attempts at Romanization that have been put forward by different groups at different times since the Qing dynasty (1644–1912). The use of pinyin was first adopted in the 1950s, and was later endorsed by the People's Republic of China as a means of improving literacy.

Do too many Romanizations spoil the broth?

Of course, like any attempt to Romanize the Chinese language, pinyin is not perfect, but it is certainly more intuitive than some of the Romanization systems that came before it. To the average person, many things about the Chinese language can seem unnecessarily complicated. Systems of Romanization are no exception. They are often a product of Chinese scholars working in dusty libraries, detached from the outside world. Because of this, many Romanization methods are at best arcane, and at worst completely incomprehensible.

稽首飲崇天主聖母

子古今人母像萬世

懷神職主

四目憐視厄娃子孫

Early Christian missionary in China

For many years English speakers have been horribly mispronouncing Chinese words and names, and not just because 'it's all Chinese to them'. The Wade-Giles system that was developed during the nineteenth century has been blamed for causing a lot of this confusion.

The Chinese 'Tao' (i.e. Taoism), as it is written in Wade-Giles Romanization, is actually pronounced with a sound closer to the English 'd', not 't'. Helpfully, it is written 'dào' in pinyin. Likewise the 'Chi' in Tai Chi (a spelling that derives from the Wade-Giles system), is in fact pronounced much closer to the English 'jee' (as in jeep). In pinyin, it is written '*tài jî*'. Some former systems live on, mostly in archaic names – for both places and people. Taipei, the capital city of Taiwan, still uses its old Wade-Giles Romanization, which is rendered as *Táiběi* in pinyin. Similarly, Mao Tse-tung and Mao Zedong are in fact the same person. No, he didn't change his name by deed poll; the difference in spelling can be explained by the varying methods of Romanization used. Thankfully, despite the odd exception, pinyin is now an international standard.

> **KEY POINTS**
> A standardized system is necessary to get rid of confusion in representing the phonetic values of Chinese characters. Take the many names of the capital, Beijing, for example:
>
> **Beijing** is the pinyin Romanization of the city's official Mandarin name.
>
> **Peip'ing** is the Wade-Giles Romanization of the old nationalist name for the city.
>
> **Peking** is the old postal system Romanization.

Confused yet? It's certainly a good job that everyone has agreed on the name 'Beijing'. At least for now...

Where pinyin falls short

Serious students are not advised to drop the study of characters and stick with pinyin alone, because it is rarely used as a proper script in itself. Written pinyin can be difficult to decipher due to the limited number of sounds in Mandarin Chinese. Consider the following story, written by Chao Yuen Ren, the Chinese-American linguist. It is composed entirely with the pinyin syllable 'shi' and its various tones.

Pinyin
Title: « *Shī Shì shí shī shǐ* »
First line: *Shíshì shīshì Shī Shì, shì shī, shì shí shí shī.*

Chinese
Title: 《施氏食獅史》
First line: 石室诗士施氏，嗜狮，誓食十狮。

English translation
Title: *Lion-Eating Poet in the Stone Den*
First line: In a stone den was a poet called Shi, who was fond of lions, and had resolved to eat ten of them.

The text is an example of classical, and not spoken, Chinese. It can be understood when written out in characters, but is almost incomprehensible in pinyin. Originally intended as an example of why Latinization of classical Chinese would not work, it is often used as an argument against Romanization in general. Characters remain the key to understanding Chinese literature, both ancient and modern.

A traditional Chinese stone lion

SHANXI OR SHAANXI?

There are two neighbouring provinces in Central/
Northern China that are both Romanized as 'Shanxi'
in pinyin – *Shānxī* 山西 and *Shǎnxī* 陕西. The only
difference between the two is the tone of the *shan*. To
avoid confusion, the latter province, in which the Shan
is pronounced with a third tone, is officially written
'Shaanxi'. It is the only official name of a Chinese
province that does not conform to the rules of pinyin.

An additional sticking point is the fact that pinyin does not represent regional dialects. It represents the sounds of Mandarin Chinese only, so pinyin relies on the widespread adoption of Mandarin. China has a number of dialects. In some areas, people from one village will not be able to understand the dialect spoken in the next village along! As you can imagine, people from different areas often found it difficult to communicate with one another until *pǔtōnghuà*, the pronunciation of the area around Beijing, was adopted as the standard pronunciation for the whole of China. Thus *pǔtōnghuà* and pinyin are interdependent. The rise of *pǔtōnghuà* and pinyin has made communication across China much simpler, but at the cost of linguistic diversity. Other Romanization systems exist for Shanghainese, Cantonese and Taiwanese, among other Chinese languages.

Pinyin: a learning tool

Although all Chinese schoolchildren learn pinyin before they go on to learn characters, don't think that it is some kind of universal script understood in all corners of China. It never fulfilled its initial purpose of replacing characters altogether. It might just be possible to order sweet and sour pork in a restaurant by writing it down in pinyin and showing it to the waiter, but as we have seen, a budding Romeo would have difficulty getting his Chinese Juliet to understand a poem composed entirely in pinyin. Granted, pinyin is found alongside characters on shop and road signs across China, but many Chinese, particularly the older generation, cannot read it. Don't forget that it wasn't until the second half of the twentieth century that it was fully introduced into the education system. Once they start learning characters, children quickly put pinyin to the back, or completely out, of their minds. It is very much a stepping stone on the path toward full literacy in Chinese.

Pinyin is also traditionally how Chinese is taught as a second language to beginners. It is a great jumping off point, teaching us how to pronounce Chinese before we start the long task of learning the characters.

If you are planning a short trip to China, then a basic knowledge of pinyin and the sounds of spoken Chinese will be enough to get by. If however you are interested in delving deeper into the language, you should consider moving on to Chinese characters – once you have a good grasp of pinyin, that is.

DID YOU KNOW?

Pinyin is used to type in Chinese on computers and mobile phones. All you have to do is type out the pinyin letters for the character you want, and a list of all characters with that pronunciation pops up. Simply choose your desired character from the list.

Brief guide to pinyin pronunciation

Chinese words are made up of one-syllable sounds, with an initial and a final. In the pinyin *xie*, to thank, the initial is 'x' and the final is 'ie'.

When looking at words in pinyin, it is important to remember that the letters of the words do not always correspond with English pronunciations. Mandarin contains some sounds which do not exist in English. Don't worry if you can't pronounce these sounds correctly first time; learning pinyin requires a fair bit of practice. Always bear in mind that a good understanding of the sounds of pinyin is the first step toward speaking good Chinese.

The following is just a rough guide to pronunciation using English language equivalents. To really perfect your spoken Chinese, find a native speaker to practise with.

Consonants
Consonants similar to their English equivalents:

f	like **f**ull
k	like **k**art
l	like **l**ate
m	like **m**an
n	like **n**ot
p	like **p**en
s	like **s**ee
t	like **t**oo
w	like **wh**at
y	like **y**es
d	like **d**o
b	like **b**ear
g	like **g**o

More difficult consonants

c	like ts in ca**ts**
ch	like ch in **ch**in, but with the mouth in a round shape and the tongue at the back of the mouth
h	like h in **h**im but with more friction in the throat (not as much as in loch)
j	like j in **j**eep but with the tongue nearer the teeth
q	like ch in **ch**eese, but with the tongue further forward
r	like r in **r**ough, but with the tongue curled upwards
sh	like sh in **sh**eep
x	somewhere between s and sh, with the tongue behind the lower front teeth, letting the air pass through
z	like ds in la**ds**
zh	like j in **j**ump, but with the tongue further back

Vowels and their combinations:

a	like a in **a**re
ai	like **eye**
ao	like ow in c**ow**
an	like an in **an**d
ang	like ang in b**ang** but with a long vowel
e	like ur in sl**ur**
ei	like ay in p**ay**
en	like en in tak**en**
eng	like ung in s**ung**
er	like **are**

i	like ee in s**ee** after most letters, but after s, z, r, c, sh, ch, zh, it sounds more like 'uh'
ia	like ya in **y**ak
iao	like yow in **yow**l
ian	like **yen**
iang	combine **y** and **ang**
ie	like ye in **ye**s
in	like in in b**in**
ing	like ing in sow**ing**
iong	combine **i** and **ong**
iu	like yo in **yo**-yo
o	like o in m**o**re
ou	like oa in b**oa**t
ong	like ong in s**ong**
u	like u in fl**u**te, but after j, q, x, or y, it sounds more like the u sound in French t**u**
ü	like the u sound in French t**u**, or ü in German **ü**ber
ua	combine **u** and **a**
uai	like **why**
ue	like **you** + **eh**
ui	like **way**
uo	combine **u** and **o**
uan	combine **u** and **an**
un	like **ooh** + **n**
uang	combine **u** and **ang**

Note that syllables are not all written separately in pinyin. Words that are made up of more than one syllable are written together, such as *pǔtōnghuà* 普通话.

COMMON MISTAKES TO AVOID

Wang: *Wang* is one of China's most common surnames, and its pronunciation is tricky for many westerners, not least because **wang** is a word in English. Forget the English slang – the 'an' should be pronounced more like 'an' in 'want' (long vowel), not the 'an' in 'fan' (short vowel).

xièxiè 谢谢 (thank you): every polite traveller learns how to say thank you in the native language of their destination, but unfortunately the pinyin '*x*' is one of the hardest sounds to make for English speakers. Forget all about the English 'x'. In fact, the syllable '*xie*' sounds a lot like 'see air' spoken very quickly. Want to say thanks in Chinese? Say 'see air, see air' as fast as you can, and you've basically got it.

ü: the ü vowel sound, similar to the 'u' of tu in French, is often confused with pinyin *u*. This can be embarrassing if for example you mix up *nǚ* 女, 'woman', with *nǔ* 弩, 'crossbow'; or confuse *lǘ* 驴, 'donkey', with *lù* 鹿, 'deer'.

Chapter 3:
Tones
声调
shēngdiào

Tones

声调
shēngdiào

At home we spoke the northern dialect, an imperfect kind of Peking dialect. But we always kept our four tones in Mandarin straight. Anybody who spoke with some other accent with other tones would sound out of tune to us.

Chao Yuen Ren

Chinese is a tonal language, and mastery over the tones is very much the key to mastery of spoken Chinese. Every Chinese character has its own set tone – although some have multiple pronunciations – and these must be learned by heart. Written characters don't give you any clues as to what tone they are pronounced in; you simply have to learn it.

There are four main tones in Mandarin Chinese: flat, rising, falling/rising, and falling. There is also a fifth neutral, unaccented tone.

The pitch of the first flat tone sounds similar to when you stick out your tongue at the doctor's and say 'ah'. This would be written ā in pinyin. The second rising tone sounds similar to the rising intonation when you ask someone, 'yes?'. The third falling/rising tone starts low, falling first before rising. This is a tricky tone as it has no real equivalent sound in English. In practice, it often sounds just like a low, falling tone. The fourth falling tone starts high and drops sharply, and is somewhat terse, like when you shout 'Look!' or 'Stop!'. The tone marks used in pinyin reflect the pitch of each respective tone. The first tone is marked by a straight, horizontal line. The second tone mark rises at an acute angle to the right. The third tone is marked by a line that dips in the middle, and the fourth by a mark falling from left to right. Tone markings are usually placed over the main vowel – *ji* 鸡 (chicken), *she* 蛇 (snake), *gou* 狗 (dog), *lu* 鹿 (deer).

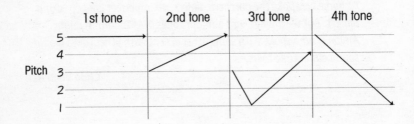

The tones of Mandarin Chinese

The four tones are represented in pinyin with tone marks. The table opposite shows tone markings above the syllable '**ba**', how the meanings of the sounds change, and a description of how each tone should sound:

Tone	Pinyin	Chinese character (example)	English	Description
1st	*bā*	八	eight	High and level
2nd	*bá*	拔	to pluck out	Rising tone
3rd	*bǎ*	靶	target	Starts low, dips down, then rises up
4th	*bà*	爸	father	Starts high, then falls sharply
neutral	*ba*	吧	(suggestion particle)	Flat, with no emphasis

What did you say about my mother?

An old chestnut of Chinese language learning is the urban legend that tone-deaf foreigners will mistakenly insult someone's mother when in conversation.

This comes from the syllable ma and its different tones: *mā* ('mother'), *má* ('hemp'), *mǎ* ('horse'), and *mà* ('scold'). As the legend goes, pronouncing all of these words as undifferentiated ma can lead to unfortunate mix-ups, such as calling someone's mother a horse, or indeed vice-versa. These words are, of course, clearly distinguished when written in Chinese characters, or when accurately pronounced in Chinese.

While this makes for a good anecdote, it is unlikely that your tones will ever get you into such hot water. Chinese people expect foreigners to have bad tones, and will generally make allowances for it. Likewise, context is important in spoken conversation, and makes accidentally insulting someone's relatives more difficult than it sounds.

USE YOUR HEAD

There are some useful body movements that can be associated with the four main tones, and can help you to memorize them.

First tone – raise your eyebrows every time you say the first high and level tone.

Second tone – tilt your head up towards the sky when you say the second rising tone. This naturally helps your tone to rise inquisitively.

Third tone – first lower your chin toward your neck, then raise your chin when you say the 3rd dipping and rising tone.

Fourth tone – nod sharply when you say the fourth falling tone. This helps accentuate the falling intonation.

These tips are particularly suited for beginners. It's probably best to stop using exaggerated movements after you become familiar with the tones.

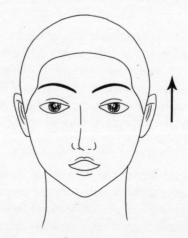

First tone

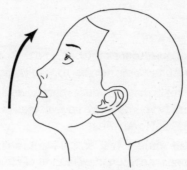

Second tone

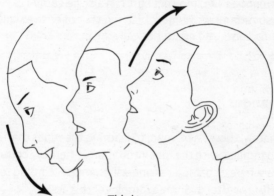

Third tone

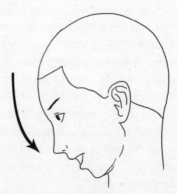

Fourth tone

> **DID YOU KNOW?**
>
> It's easy to get one's tones confused, and this can lead to amusing results. Some notable tone mix-ups:
>
> Foreign diplomats may introduce themselves as *wàijiāoguǎn* 外胶管, 'rubber hosing', instead of *wàijiāogūan* 外交官, 'diplomat'.
>
> Saying *wǒ yào shuìjiào* 我要睡觉, 'I want to sleep', with the wrong tones can result in *wǒ yào shuǐjiǎo* 我要水饺, 'I want dumplings'. Not quite the same thing!
>
> A *wǎngba* 网吧, 'internet bar', can also be easily mispronounced *wángbā* 王八, which is offensive slang for tortoise, and metaphorically means 'cuckold'.

Tone changes

Unfortunately, there's a bit more to learning the tones than just becoming familiar with the four intonations. There are certain situations where a character's tone will change according to what comes before or after it. Some examples of this are:

- When two third tones come together, to save the speaker from tonal gymnastics, the first third tone becomes closer to a second tone. In this case, *kěyǐ* 可以, 'to be able', becomes *kéyǐ*.
- The character *bù* 不 'no' is normally fourth tone, except when it is followed by another fourth tone, when it turns into a second tone. Examples: *búduì* 不对, 'incorrect', and *búcuò* 不错, 'not bad'.
- The character *yī* 一, 'one', is originally first tone, but like *bù* 不, it can change tone in certain situations. It remains first tone when used by itself, if used at the end of the sentence, and when used as a numeral such as *èrshíyī* 二十一, '21'. However, its tone changes in some cases, such as the following:

a) Directly before the fourth tone, *yī* 一 becomes second tone. For example: *yíyàng* 一样, 'the same', *yícì* 一次, 'once'.
b) Directly before the first, second, and third tones, *yi* 一 becomes fourth tone. For example: *yìnián* 一年, 'one year', *yìqǐ* 一起, 'together'.

Tones require patience

Getting the tones right is very important. If you use the wrong tones, your listeners may either not be able to understand you, or snicker at your mistakes. Non-native speakers tend to confuse the first tone with the fourth, and the second tone with the third. It can be frustrating for learners when their Mandarin is misunderstood simply because their tones are a little off, but this is a fact of life for non-native speakers. Patience and slow, clear repetition can help to overcome this obstacle.

Above all, don't be scared off by the tones. It may all sound very alien at first, but remember that English also happens to be a highly inflected language. The whole meaning of a sentence in English can be changed by a slight change in tone and emphasis too!

DID YOU KNOW?
Researchers have found a strong link between speaking a tonal language – such as Chinese or Vietnamese – and having perfect pitch. Knowing Chinese won't turn you into the next Pavarotti, but it just might help you to recognize musical notes and sing in key.

Chapter 4:
Numbers and money
数字与金钱
shùzì yǔ jīnqián

Numbers and money

数字与金钱
shùzì yǔ jīnqián

The Tao produced One;
One produced Two;
Two produced Three;
Three produced All things.
Laozi

The importance of numbers

China is a numerologist's paradise. Wherever you go in China, there are numbers: they are not just found on clock faces, in calendars, and phone directories. They are not only used to count. They are also deeply embedded in Chinese language and culture. Some numbers can bring good fortune, others calamity. Someone who is described as having 'three heads and six arms' (*sāntóu liùbì* 三头六臂) is capable and gets things done; and one who 'disowns their six relations' (*liùqīn bùrèn* 六亲不认) is heartless and cold.

China's scenic spots bombard the visitor with an overload of numbers and statistics. Upon entering the majestic Forbidden City in Beijing, one of the first things visitors are informed of is the exact number of buildings and rooms it houses – 980 buildings and 8,704 rooms, if you must know. Ancient books were written in chapters in accordance with the principles of numerology, and weddings and important events are held on dates that will bring good fortune. This obsession with numbers is perhaps fitting for the world's most populous country.

Counting

Although numbers hold a special power in China, counting is still their primary purpose. Basic greetings and pleasantries aside, numbers are perhaps the most useful vocabulary items for any student of the language to know.

one	*yī*	一
two	*èr*	二
three	*sān*	三
four	*sì*	四
five	*wǔ*	五
six	*liù*	六
seven	*qī*	七
eight	*bā*	八
nine	*jiǔ*	九
ten	*shí*	十

- Eleven is expressed as 'ten-one', *shíyī* 十一, while twelve is 'ten-two', *shíèr* 十二, etc.
- Twenty is expressed as 'two–ten', *èrshí* 二十, while thirty is 'three-ten', *sānshí* 三十, etc.
- Twenty-one is expressed as 'two-ten-one', *èrshíyī* 二十一, while twenty-two is 'two-ten-two', *èrshíèr* 二十二, etc.
- One hundred is *yībǎi* 一百, and one thousand is *yīqiān* 一千

So far, so straightforward. Sadly, things get trickier with larger numbers, because the Chinese orders of magnitude are slightly different to those used in English.

- *wàn* 万 ten thousand: Chinese has no single word for million. To express one million, you say *yībǎiwàn* 一百万 or literally 'one hundred ten thousands'. The Chinese word for millionaire is, therefore, *baíwànfùwēng* 百万富翁 – literally 'one hundred ten thousands rich person'.
- *yì* 亿 one hundred million: similarly, Chinese does not have a word for billion. Instead, the Chinese count by hundred million. *Yì* 亿 is hundred million, so billion is *shíyì* 十亿 or literally 'ten hundred millions'.

> ### *chéngqiān chéngwàn* 成千成万
> This is an idiom meaning 'thousands upon thousands'. Literally translated, it reads 'in thousands and tens of thousands'.

Like most things in Chinese, to become fluent with larger numbers you really need to start **thinking** in the language. Think in terms of **ten thousands** and **hundred millions**, otherwise you will constantly be trying to convert the number in your head, which can lead to mistakes.

> ### NUMBER GESTURES
> Chinese people have a way of using the digits on one hand to express the numbers one to ten. These are often used in day-to-day life, for example at the wet market, in shops, and during dice games.

Numbers one to five are straightforward (if you have a full complement of digits).

Six (六)
The little finger and thumb are extended, with the other fingers closed into the palm. Although this looks like a bull's horns, turn it upside down and you can see the resemblance of the bottom half of the Chinese character for six.

Seven (七)
Touch all your fingertips together, with the fingers pointing downward; or alternatively just bring the fingertips of the thumb and first two fingers together.

Eight (八)
The thumb and index finger make a sideways 'L', other fingers closed, with the palm facing the onlooker.

Nine (九)
Make a hook with the index finger, keeping the other fingers closed. This resembles the 'hook' in the Chinese character for nine.

Ten (十)
There are two ways of depicting the number ten: either with a closed fist, or with the middle finger of one hand crossing an extended index finger on the other hand, like an impromptu crucifix.

Chinese number gestures

Did you know...?

Chinese students are said to outperform those from Western countries on maths tests and other numerical tasks. What makes the difference? Some suggest that Chinese speakers can memorize more numbers than English speakers in the same amount of time. Chinese students may be able to memorize numbers faster because of the way the words sound in their head. The Chinese words for the first nine numbers are all short and concise, like bullet points. Take *yī*, *èr*, *sān*, and *bā*, for example – they average out at about a quarter of a second each when spoken. Although some basic digits in English are equally short – 'one' and 'two', for example – 'three' is a little longer and 'seven' is comparatively slow to say, as it has two syllables. Studies suggest that English numbers average at a third of a second each, making English-speakers work harder when memorizing them.

Helpful hint

One: *yī/yāo*

The number one in Chinese is *yī*. When part of a larger number that is read aloud, such as a phone or passport number, it is normally pronounced *yāo*. This is to avoid confusion with the number seven, *qī*, which sounds similar to one, *yī*.

Two: *èr/liǎng*

The number two, when in isolation, as an ordinal, or part of a longer number, is *èr* 二. When we want to say two of something, we say *liǎng* 两.

For example: *dìèrtiān* 第二天, 'the second day'; *liǎng gè píngguǒ* 两个苹果, 'two apples'.

In modern slang, èr in Mandarin Chinese can mean 'imbecile'. The sentence *nǐ hěn èr* 你很二 means 'you are stupid'. Additionally, *èrbǎiwǔ*, literally 250, is used as an insult to mean 'fool'. To avoid this, you can say *liǎngbǎiwǔ* – just another wording for 250 that avoids using *èr*.

Internet slang

Numbers are increasingly used in text messages and over the internet as a quick and informal way of communicating.

- The number *bābā* 88 stands in for *bāibāi* 拜拜, itself slang for 'bye bye'. A good equivalent for this in English would be the internet slang 'l8er'.
- A number of 5s – *wǔwǔwǔ* 555– can imitate a sobbing noise, *wūwūwū* 呜呜呜.
- Numbers can also be strung together to imitate sentences. *Wǔyāobā* 518 can mean 'I want to get rich' (loosely following the sounds of *wǒyàofā* '我要发'), and *Wǔèryī* 521 can mean 'I love you' (*wǒàinǐ* 我爱你).

Not just a numbers game

While we can agree that in the West the number 13 is considered to be unlucky, and seven is generally lucky, English-speaking countries have very few other universally lucky or unlucky numbers. China, on the other hand, has a whole laundry list.

Most numbers in China are today considered either lucky or unlucky based on the way that they sound. If they sound like another word in Chinese that means something 'good', such as 'long-life', then they are considered lucky. If they sound like something bad, like 'death', then they are unlucky. Chinese has a relatively small number of sounds, which makes these associations possible (not a lot sounds like 'seven' in English, for example).

One

In recent years, the number **one** has come to represent the state of being single. 11 November (11/11) is a newly-celebrated grass-roots festival known as Singles' Day in China. On this day, single people will get together for a meal, or attend such activities as blind-date parties.

Two

The number **two** is generally considered to be a good number in Chinese culture, if not particularly lucky. It is common to use double symbols, such as the character *xǐ* 囍, 'double happiness', as an indicator of good fortune. In addition, two can symbolize husband and wife, heaven and earth, and the yin and yang.

Three

The number **three** sounds similar to the character for 'birth' (*shēng* 生), and in the ancient Taoist classics, three was said to be the number that 'produced all things'. It symbolizes the family unit of father, mother, and child. The character *xīn* 鑫, normally used in names, symbolizes wealth and prosperity, and is composed of the character for 'gold', *jīn* 金, repeated three times. Three can represent plenty, and is considered a lucky number.

Four

The number **four** is bad news in China, and people go out of their way to avoid it. Four (*sì* 四) is considered an unlucky number in Chinese because it sounds almost the same as the word for 'death' (*sǐ* 死). Because of this, some buildings don't have a fourth floor, just like some buildings in the Western world avoid having a 13th floor, and people try to attain phone numbers with as few fours as possible. Four has not always been seen as a bringer of bad luck. Ancient Chinese believed even numbers to be lucky, and this includes the number four. The number four represents the four seasons, and so is symbolic of wholeness. Most chengyu idioms in Chinese are composed of four characters, and this is known as the *sìzìgé* 四字格, the 'four character structure'. The compass directions are known as the *sìfāng* 四方, the 'four sides'; ancient cities had *sìjiāo* 四郊, the 'four districts' or suburbs, and women in ancient China had to abide by the *sìdé* 四德, the 'four virtues'. These virtues were: morality, *dé* 德; physical charm, *róng* 容; propriety in speech, *yán* 言; and efficiency in needlework, *gōng* 功.

Five

While not considered either particularly lucky or unlucky, **five** is used as a number that symbolically encapsulates all things of a certain field or subject. For example, the *wǔdú* 五毒, 'five poisons', are: the scorpion, snake, centipede, gecko, and toad, but can refer to all poisonous beasts; and the *wǔgǔ* 五谷, 'five grains', are: rice, corn, millet, wheat, and beans, but can refer to food crops in general.

Tracing this principle back to its roots, it is no surprise to learn that five is most often associated with the five elements in ancient Chinese philosophy (water, fire, earth, wood, and metal): the elements that make up the entire universe. There are also five primary colours – blue, red, white, black, and yellow, which are themselves associated with the five elements, and the five directions (north, south, east, west, and centre), among other things. In Chinese numerology, the numbers one and two represent wood, three and four fire, five and six earth, seven and eight metal, and nine and ten water.

There are hundreds of *chéngyǔ* idioms that contain the number five. A couple of examples would be: *wǔtǐ tóudì* 五体投地, to prostrate one's five body parts [four limbs and head], which means 'to be in utter admiration', and *xuéfù wǔchē* 学富五车, to have read five cartloads of books, which means 'to be very learned'.

Six

In Mandarin, the number **six** is a lucky number: it is pronounced *liu*, and sounds similar to *liú* 流, flow, which is considered good for money-making. It indicates 'a constant flowing stream' of business.

> *liùliù dàshùn* 六六大顺
> This idiom means 'everything according to one's wishes', but literally means 'six six great favour'. Two sixes is considered lucky because the *kūn* 坤 hexagram from the *Book of Changes* is composed of 12 lines, in two columns of six (or six broken lines). It is a sign of good fortune.

Seven

The number **seven** has long held a special importance for Chinese Taoists – the seven stars that form the Big Dipper are said to be able to control the forces of heaven and earth. Throughout Chinese history, the number seven has been associated with good things – the group of Taoist scholars who came together in the third century AD were known as the *zhúlín qīxián* 竹林七贤, the 'seven sages of the bamboo grove', and the seven daughters of the Jade Emperor were collectively called the 'seven celestial maidens', *qī xiānnǚ* 七仙女. The number seven is also closely associated with the Chinese equivalent of Valentine's Day – the seventh day of the seventh month of the lunar calendar, or *qīxījié* 七夕节.

Eight

The word for **eight**, *bā*, sounds similar to the Chinese word for 'prosper' or 'get rich' (*fā* 发—short for *fācái* 发财). The number eight is viewed as such an auspicious number that any number with several eights is considered very lucky. Phone numbers containing a number of eights are very valuable, highly-prized possessions, as are car licence plates consisting of many 8s. The general rule is simple: the more eights the better. The telephone hotline for the theatrical performance *Impression: Lijiang*, held at the foot of the Jade Dragon Mountain in southwestern Yunnan province, may be China's luckiest phone number – 0888 8888888.

> **DID YOU KNOW?**
> One of China's most expensive car numberplates, 浙 (*Zhè*)C 88888, registered in the coastal city of Wenzhou in China's southeastern Zhejiang province, was bought in 2006 for RMB 1.6 million. The number obviously didn't bring its owner much luck, as he was forced to sell the car, along with the numberplate, in 2010 after getting into a large amount of debt.

Consider that the opening ceremony of the 2008 Summer Olympics in Beijing began on 8 August 2008, at eight seconds and eight minutes past eight pm local time. The association between eight and good luck is not just folk superstition; it is endorsed at the highest levels of government. Not everything to do with the number eight is good news, however. China's imperial examinations during the Ming and Qing dynasties placed great emphasis on a style of essay known as the *bāgǔwén* 八股文, literally 'eight legged essay', which was a nightmare for examinees. So named for its eight parts, the eight-legged essays became synonymous with pedantry and lack of innovation.

Nine

The number **nine** was historically associated with the emperor of China, and the number was frequently used in matters relating to the Son of Heaven. Imperial Palaces in the Forbidden City were built to be 99 feet tall, and even the doornails were arranged in rows of nine. One of the cruellest punishments the emperor could bestow upon a wrongdoer was the 'nine familial exterminations', *zhūlián jiŭzú* 株连 九族, whereby an offender's entire family from great- great- grandfather to great- great- grandson would be put to death.

The number nine and its multiplications feature prominently in Chinese culture. Nine was traditionally seen as the 'largest' number, and signified completion. It sounds the same as *jiŭ* 久, 'longevity', and is thus prized as a lucky number that blesses long life. In ancient China, men of letters and emperors alike looked up to the number nine. The high heavens were spread across *jiŭxiāo* 九霄, 'nine levels', officials were sorted into *jiŭpǐn* 九品, 'nine ranks', and Chinese territory was divided into *jiŭzhōu* 九州, 'nine states'.

The number nine is also featured in its fair share of four-character idioms. For example, *sānguì jiŭkòu* 三跪九叩, literally 'to kneel three times and kowtow nine times', refers to the formal etiquette observed upon meeting the emperor. *Yīyán jiŭdǐng* 一言九鼎, literally 'one word is worth nine sacred tripods', is used to express words that carry enormous weight.

Multiples of nine appear throughout Chinese literature as culturally significant numbers. The Buddhist monk Xuanzang, who legendarily journeyed to the West to seek out Buddhist scriptures, endured 81 hardships on his travels. A total of 108 generals appear in *The Water Margin*, one of China's four classic novels. Ancient China's military tactics can be summed up by the '36 stratagems', and the traditional weapons of Chinese martial arts fall into the '18 kinds of weapons', *shíbābān wǔyì* 十八般武艺.

72: an important number?

The number 72 is one of great significance in China, and one of the more crucial multiples of nine. It crops up in a variety of places: the Monkey King (*Sūn Wùkōng* 孙悟空) in Chinese legend has control of over 72 transformations, allowing him to turn into various animals and objects (although not people; as he would always be given away by his tail). The great sage Confucius had 72 famous disciples. *Liu Bang*, the first Han emperor, was said to have had 72 moles on his left thigh. Ancient Chinese divided the 365 days of the year into 72 distinct periods, and 72 is also the number of the Immortals of the Taoist religion. The origins of the significance of this number can be traced back to the *Book of Changes*, the ancient classic of divination. The *Book of Changes* details the eight trigrams, composed of three broken or unbroken lines. There are a possible combination of 64 hexagrams, each made up of six lines. If we add 64 and eight, we get 72.

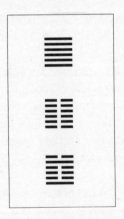

Three hexagrams from the Book of Changes

The Book of Changes

The *Book of Changes* is one of China's oldest classic texts, and represents the origins of Chinese numerology. It contains 64 hexagrams, each associated with a different oracle, and used for purposes of divination. Each of the 64 hexagrams found in the *Book of Changes* has a different description that is interpreted by the diviner. The broken lines of the hexagrams are 'yin', the unbroken lines are 'yang'. Yin represents things that are female, earthly, and passive, while yang represents things that are male, heavenly, and active. Professional diviners refer to yang lines as 'nine' and yin lines as 'six'.

Divinations are made by generating a hexagram at random and reading the corresponding divination text from the book. An easy way of generating a hexagram is to use three coins, determining the lines of a hexagram by the number of heads or tails that are thrown. The ancients used a pot of yarrow stalks to generate the hexagrams, but this method is more complex and less readily accessible than the coin method that is more often used today.

Dates

In Chinese, numbers are also used to count the days of the week and months of the year. This makes learning dates particularly easy. Monday is *xīngqīyī* 星期一, literally 'week one' or the 'first day of the week'. Tuesday is *xīngqīèr* 星期二, the 'second day of the week', Wednesday is *xīngqīsān* 星期三, Thursday *xīngqīsì* 星期四, Friday *xīngqīwǔ* 星期五 and Saturday *xīngqīliù* 星期六. The only day of the week that doesn't follow this logic is Sunday, *xīngqītiān* 星期天, also called *xīngqīrì* 星期日. Because *rì* 日 is sun in Chinese, *xīngqīrì* 星期日 literally means 'the day of the sun', just like the English Sunday.

For the days of the week, *xīngqī* can be replaced by *zhōu* 周 or *lǐbài* 礼拜: for example *zhōuyī* 周一 or *lǐbàiyī* 礼拜一, both also meaning 'Monday'. Note that you **cannot** say *zhōutiān* 周天 for Sunday, you can only use *zhōurì* 周日. Both *lǐbàitiān* 礼拜天 and *lǐbàirì* 礼拜日 are acceptable as well.

Months (*yuè* 月) are also very easy to memorize. January is *yīyuè* 一月, the 'first month'. February is *èryuè* 二月, the 'second month'. March is *sānyuè* 三月, and so on, to December, which is *shíèr yuè* 十二月, the 'twelfth month'.

Numbers in years (*nián* 年) are read out one-by-one, with the word for year after the last number. For example, 2012 is read 'two zero one two year', or *èr líng yī èr nián* 二零一二年. Dates in Chinese are written from the year to the day, starting with the largest units (years) and getting smaller, just like addresses. For example, '24 December 2012' would be written: *èr líng yī èr nián shíèr yuè èrshísì rì*, 2012 年12月24日.

> **DID YOU KNOW?**
> The calendar year in Taiwan is calculated from the founding of the Republic of China government in 1912. Mainland China uses the modern Gregorian calendar for official business.

Money

China's currency is known as the people's currency: *rénmínbì* 人民币. It has held this title since 1949. It is legal tender on the Chinese mainland, but not in Hong Kong or Macau, where the Hong Kong Dollar and the Macanese Pataca are used, respectively.

The basic unit of currency is the **yuan** (written as *yuán* 元, but deriving from *yuán* 圓) which literally means 'round', after the shape of the coins. One *yuán* is equal to about 10 pence sterling or 15 cents USD. The *yuán* is divided into ten *jiǎo* 角, colloquially known as *máo* 毛, and one *máo* is further divided into ten *fēn* 分. *Fēn* are rarely used in modern China as their value is so low. *Yuán* are commonly known as *kuài* 块, 'lump', in modern slang. This was originally a way of referring to pieces of silver. For example: *wǒ dōuli zhǐyǒu wǔshí kuài* 我兜里只有五十块, 'I've only got fifty bucks on me'.

Yuán is used in Chinese as a translation for the word 'dollar', so the US dollar is called *Měiyuán* 美元. The word *yuán* is also used as a translation for many different currencies around the world. The Japanese yen is the *rìyuán* 日元, 'Japanese yuan', and the Korean won is the *hányuán* 韩元, or 'Korean yuan'. The Euro is called the *ōuyuán* (欧元), or 'European yuan'.

IDENTIFY ANTIQUE COINS

Coins of the Qing Dynasty (1644–1911) generally carried the era name of the emperor, for example *Kāngxī* 康熙, and the name of the currency (in this case *tōngbǎo* 通宝, meaning 'general currency'), on the top side. The mint location where the coins were cast can be found on the bottom side.

Qing dynasty coin

IDENTIFY MODERN BANKNOTES

Mainland Chinese banknotes in current circulation have a portrait of Chairman Mao on the front side and depictions of famous national landmarks on the reverse. These are:

1 *yuán*: Pagodas on the surface of West Lake in Hangzhou

5 *yuán*: Mount Tai in Shandong, the easternmost of China's five sacred mountains

10 *yuán*: Three Gorges on the Yangtze

20 *yuán*: Karst mountain scenery around the Li River in Guilin

50 *yuán*: The Potala palace in Lhasa, Tibet, ancestral seat of the Dalai Lama

100 *yuán*: The Great Hall of the People in Beijing

Haggling

In China's marketplaces, where goods aren't labelled in price, you're positively expected to haggle.

HOW TO HAGGLE

1. Ask *duōshǎo qián?* 多少钱?, 'How much is it?'

2. The seller will name a price. It's important to remember that this is not what they expect to get, or what the item is actually worth. It is merely what they hope you will pay.

3. Offer one fifth of the price (or even less, depending on the situation). This is not a realistic final price, but simply a platform from which to begin haggling.

4. If the seller doesn't budge, try the age-old tactic of 'walking away', and the seller may well run after you, shouting a better price.

5. Continue the back and forth, and see if you can settle on a suitable price.

It helps to know the relative value of what you want to buy, but this may not always be possible in China. Basically, if you end up paying a price that you are comfortable with, then you've done fine.

DID YOU KNOW?

Discounts in China are known as *zhékòu* 折扣. When talking about discounts in English, we mention how much money is saved, i.e. '10 per cent off', or '20 per cent off'. In China, it's the other way around: one says how much of the original price is left, for example a 10 per cent discount in Chinese is *jiǔzhé* 九折, literally 'discounted to 90 per cent'. Likewise, 20 per cent off would be *bāzhé* 八折, 'discounted to 80 per cent', and so on.

LANGUAGE TIP:

Here are some useful phrases that can help you while shopping in China.

Tàiguìle! 太贵了!, 'Too expensive!'

Néng piányi diǎn ma? 能便宜点吗?, 'Can it be a little cheaper?'

Néng shuākǎ ma? 能刷卡吗?, 'Can I pay by credit card?'

Zhège shì jiǎde! Zěnme zhème guì! 这个是假的! 怎么这么贵!, 'This is fake! Why is it so expensive?'

Chapter 5:
Chinese characters
汉字
Hànzì

Chinese characters

汉字
Hànzì

The Yellow Emperor's Court Recorder, Cangjie, looked down and saw the tracks left by the birds and the beasts. He realized that by distinguishing their patterns he was able to differentiate one from the other. Thus writing was born.

Xu Shen

The Chinese character has long been a source of mystery and fascination for those who speak languages with an alphabet. Ever since China caught the popular imagination in the late nineteenth century, people in the West have been wondering as to the rhyme and reason behind the strange signs of its written language.

Cangjie, legendary creator of Chinese writing

Chinese legend has it that a court official of the Yellow Emperor, Cangjie 仓颉, created writing. He was said to have been six foot tall, with four eyes and four pupils. He could see all things, such as the courses of the stars in the heavens.

In ancient times, people used to tie knots in lengths of rope as a way of remembering things. The Yellow Emperor was dissatisfied with this primitive method, and asked Cangjie to come up with something better. Cangjie went outside, and looking at the birds in the sky and the beasts on the ground, created characters that had the characteristics of the things they represented. So it was that early pictographs were born. The raised platform where Cangjie first looked about him and put pen to paper – or perhaps more accurately chisel to stone – can still be visited today, some 15 kilometres southwest of the modern-day city of Xi'an.

This is of course just a legend, and we cannot attribute the creation of Chinese characters to just one man. What we do know is that Chinese characters have had a sweeping influence across Asia and beyond: they used to be the national script for Vietnam, and are still used to different degrees in Japan, Korea, and throughout China. There are over twenty varieties of Chinese script used around the world, and even when not used for purposes of communication, they are held in high regard for their artistic value.

The Chinese character is the carrier of a written tradition that has been preserved for thousands of years. A modern schoolboy can take up a copy of a text attributed to Confucius, who lived some 2,500 years ago, and read it aloud, with little to no special training. Admittedly, the schoolboy would still require the text to be explained for him to have any understanding of its meaning. Yet despite their thousands of years of history, scholars still have difficulty agreeing what to call the characters themselves. In their modern form they are not 'pictographs', nor are they 'hieroglyphics', as they are not recognizable pictures. Others have suggested 'logographs', and even 'sinographs': this is because the characters are symbols that represent Chinese words. For our purposes, 'Chinese characters' will do.

Characters are really what make Chinese a difficult language. It's not just foreign learners who think this, either: Chinese people believe it too. They find their own language hard to master, which makes them gasp in wonder at the achievement of any foreigner who can scale the 'Great Wall of Chinese'.

> **DID YOU KNOW?**
> The Chinese version of the phrase 'it's all Greek to me', i.e. something that is too difficult to understand, is *xiàng tiānshū yíyàng* 像天书一样, meaning 'it's like heavenly script'. It follows then that the Chinese don't believe that any other earthly language is as difficult as theirs.

Origins

Scholars are unsure how far back Chinese writing can be traced, but the earliest characters used as a form of writing are probably the Oracle bone script. The oracle bones date back to over 1,000 years BC, and are primarily records of fortune-telling divinations held for the rulers of the Shang Dynasty (1600–1045 BC). The bones, normally tortoise shells or ox shoulder blades, were inscribed with a question, and then heated until cracks appeared. The diviner would look at the lines formed by the cracks and make the reading based upon their shape.

The oracle bones were first discovered by a Qing dynasty government official at the end of the nineteenth century. The official was suffering from malaria, and a friend brought him some 'dragon bones' to grind up as medicine. The sick man noticed that there were characters that had been inscribed onto the bone, and recognized it as an early form of writing. Ever since this discovery, the oracle bones have been in high demand by antique collectors and linguists alike. The sad fact is, nobody knows how many valuable examples of oracle bones have been ground up and subsequently digested over the centuries.

Types of Chinese character

Xu Shen (c. 58–147AD), an ancient Chinese linguist, is generally recognized as the first person to organize Chinese characters into distinct categories. Below are some of the more common types.

Pictographs

The easiest category to recognize; these are the characters that evolved from primitive drawings of the objects that they are supposed to represent. The ancients wanted to write 'sun', so they drew a picture of a sun. Over time, the pictographs have become more stylized, but some are still recognisable today.

Only a small fraction of Chinese characters fall into this category. Some people who don't know much about Chinese think that you can look at a Chinese sentence and make an educated guess as to its meaning, because they're 'just drawings'. This is completely untrue. Take the simple sentence:

rén jiàn mǎ 人見馬 (in traditional characters)

Can you guess what this means?

Answer: 'person sees horse'

Here you can see the person standing on two legs (*rén* 人). Then, his eyes cast about, moving – an eye (stylized, *mù* 目) on top of two legs, making 'see' (*jiàn* 见). He sees a horse, standing on its four legs (*mǎ* 马). It's clear that even this very simple sentence would be impossible to guess without the above explanation.

Most Chinese characters are not pictographs. Even back in the time of the oracle bone characters, the earliest form of Chinese writing, only around a quarter of the characters were pictographic.

Examples of some pictographs: *rì* 日 (sun); *yuè* 月 (moon); *mù* 木 (tree); *rén* 人 (person).

Simple ideograms

While drawing a picture of a person when you want to write 'person' is easy for us to understand, pictographs aren't ideal for representing abstract ideas, as any good Pictionary player will tell you. Try writing 'ontological theory' in pictures. To represent abstract ideas, simple ideograms were formed. These characters are visual representations of non-concrete ideas.

The simplest of these is *yī* 一, 'one', a single line representing the idea of 'one'. The easiest characters for any beginner to learn are the first three numbers: 'one' (*yī* 一), 'two' (*èr* 二) and 'three' (*sān* 三), because they are the simplest of the simple ideograms. Another example would be 'up' (*shàng* 上). The bottom line represents a level, with the top part indicating the idea of 'above', or 'up'.

Characters in this category can also be alterations of existing pictographs, after which they take on a new meaning. Take *běn* 本, 'root', for example. The character is an alteration of the pictogram for 'tree', *mù* 木. There is an extra line at the bottom of the graph, indicating 'root' – that which is found at the base of the tree.

Similarly, the character *mò* 末, 'end', shows a line at the top of the tree, indicating the tip. Another simple ideogram is 'blade', *rèn* 刃, which shows an extra mark added onto the pictogram for 'knife', *dāo* 刀, indicating the knife's edge.

Associative compounds

These characters may sound complicated, but are in fact extremely simple. They are formed from two or more characters that combine to create a new meaning. The most well-trodden examples of this would be the combinations of the character for 'tree', *mù* 木. Two trees combined form a 'wood', *lín* 林, while three trees combined make a 'forest', *sēn* 森.

In a similar fashion, the character *rén* 人 means 'person'. When two are combined, we get *cóng* 从, which means 'to follow', as in one person following behind another. Three people together make *zhòng* 众, or 'crowd', showing that in Chinese, three really is a crowd.

Phono-semantic compounds

The majority of Chinese characters fall into this category. They are composed of two parts: a pictographic element that offers clues as to the meaning of the character, and a phonetic element that offers clues as to how it is pronounced. An example of this would be *hú* 湖, 'lake'. The character is composed of a water radical, *sāndiǎnshuǐ* 三点水 (literally 'three dots of water') on the left, and *hú* 胡, which is the phonetic part, on the right.

Knowing how the characters are put together helps us to learn them more effectively.

> ***fāngkuàizì* 方块字**
> The Chinese language has another name for Chinese characters: *fāngkuài zì* 方块字, literally 'square characters'. Each character should occupy the same amount of space – a square – and no matter how many strokes it contains, it should not be enlarged in relation

to other, less complex characters. When learning characters, Chinese students practise by writing on special paper printed with square boxes. Consider that *xíng* 行, 'to travel', is a single character, but its component parts are also separate characters in themselves. The left part, *chì* 彳, means 'to step with the left foot', and the right part, *chù* 亍, means 'to step with the right foot'. When these characters come together they form the two-character word *chìchù* 彳亍, which means 'to walk slowly'. Because the individual characters should be in the centre of their respective 'squares', the gap in between tells us that these are two different characters, and not *xíng* 行.

Composition of a character

Radicals

Radicals, *bùshǒu* 部首 in Chinese, are the components of Chinese characters, the building blocks by which they can be identified. Radicals are what we use to look characters up in Chinese dictionaries. A radical may point to the meaning of a character (as in the examples below), but this is not always the case.

Some important radicals:

- Water: *sāndiǎnshuǐ* 三点水

Characters with this radical usually have something to do with water: *jiāng* 江 (river), *hú* 湖 (lake), *hóng* 洪 (flood)

- Tree: *mùzìpáng* 木字旁

Characters with this radical often have something to do with wood or trees: *cái* 材 (timber), *cūn* 村 (village), *shān* 杉 (fir tree)

- Vertical heart: *jiānxīnpáng* 竖心旁

Characters with this radical, known as the 'vertical heart' because it looks like the character for 'heart' (*xīn* 心) on its side, often have something to do with feelings and affairs of the heart: *lián* 怜 (pity), *huǐ* 悔 (regret), *hèn* 恨 (hate)

DIFFERENT WORDS FOR JADE

When we think of China, the material, **jade**, is one of the first things that comes to mind. After all, the 'jade empire' is another word for imperial China. In ancient times, the character for 'jade', *yù* 玉, was almost indistinguishable from that of *wáng* 王, 'king', with the extra dot being added later as a way of separating the two. Jade has long been a symbol of the emperor's wealth and power, and the emperor would use jade utensils in his daily life, from jade bowls and chopsticks to imperial seals carved from the ornamental stone. The close links between jade culture and Chinese language are reflected by the sheer number of characters related to jade that can be found in the language.

A brief selection of words to do with jade: *kē* 珂 'jade-like stone'; *dīnglíng* 玎玲 'the tinkling sound made by jade pendants'; *lín* 琳 'beautiful jade'; *guī* 珪 'jade tablet'; *mào* 瑁 'imperial jade'; *cóng* 琮 'octagonal jade object'; *dì* 瑅 'white jade worn on the belt'.

Notice that all these characters share the same radical: the 'jade radical' (*yùzìpáng* 玉字旁), which is actually written as a 'king radical' (*wángzìpáng* 王字旁).

Strokes

Now that we know how the characters are grouped, how are they constructed in the first place? Chinese characters are constructed from simple units called 'strokes', or *bǐhuà* 笔划. The strokes are generally made with a single continuous motion of the pen. There are three general categories of strokes: dots, lines, and hooks, but these can be further subdivided.

When talking about characters, it is common to talk about how many strokes they contain. All characters are composed of strokes, and Chinese dictionaries arrange characters by their number of strokes. The simplest character in Chinese has only one stroke, it is the word *yī* 一, the number 'one', and is simply written as a horizontal line.

In contrast, one of the most complex characters contains 64 strokes; it is a rare word pronounced as *zhè*, meaning 'verbose'.

The character zhè

Stroke order

Characters should be written in the correct sequence, known as stroke order. If you get the order wrong it can throw your characters off balance; Chinese people will notice, and likely comment on it.

Not to worry, however, as there are only two basic rules that should be followed:

1. Top before bottom. When writing the character *sān* 三 (three), you start with the top horizontal line and continue down, finishing with the bottom line.
2. Left before right. When writing the character *bā* 八 (eight), for example, you start with the left diagonal stroke, and finish with the right diagonal stroke.

The Eight Principles of Yong (*yǒngzì bāfǎ* 永字八法)

It is said that in the Eastern Jin dynasty (317–420 AD), the calligrapher Wang Xizhi dedicated several years of his life to perfecting the character *yǒng* 永, 'eternal'. He believed that in order to write this one character, one must use all eight brush strokes of the Regular Script. If one could grasp the principles of these eight brush strokes, then one would be able to write any character. In a way then, this one character held the key to mastering Chinese calligraphy. Wang Xizhi passed on these 'Eight Principles of Yong' to his grandchildren, who kept the tradition alive, and Chinese children still learn them in schools today. These are the eight strokes, with Wang's own poetic names for them in brackets:

1. The dot, written with a small diagonal stroke (strange stone, *guàishí* 怪石)
2. The horizontal stroke, from right to left (jade table, *yù'àn* 玉案)
3. The downward stroke (iron pillar, *tiězhù* 铁柱)
4. The hook, that is attached to other strokes (crab's pincer, *xièzhuǎ* 蟹爪)
5. Flick to the right (tiger's tooth, *hǔyá* 虎牙)
6. The delicate, tapering curve (rhinoceros' horn, *xījiǎo* 犀角)
7. The downwards slant to the left (pecking bird, *niǎozhuó* 鸟啄)
8. The downwards stroke to the right, with a sharp finish (golden knife, *jīndāo* 金刀)

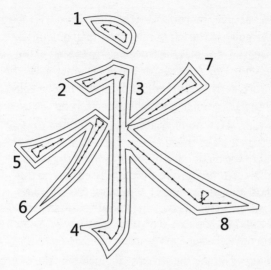

The eight principles of Yong

HOW TO USE A CHINESE DICTIONARY

Nothing illustrates the tortuous difficulties of the Chinese script more than the process of looking up Chinese characters in a dictionary. It can be a time-consuming exercise, often fraught with frustration. To the uninitiated, the process seems like some arcane ritual that requires the alignment of the planets and a sacrifice to the ancient Taoist gods to accomplish. Like so many things, however, once you have grasped the basics, it becomes a fairly routine – if still lengthy – process. Looking up a character in a Chinese dictionary requires some knowledge of radicals and strokes.

Looking up '家'

Let's say we come across the character 家, and not recognizing it, decide to look it up in a dictionary. Examine the character and identify its radical.

This is actually more difficult than it sounds. The radical is normally on the left of the character: For *làng* 浪, 'wave', the radical is the three dots to the left of the character, signifying water. For our character, 家, the radical is at the top of the character, the 'roof'. If you can't identify a radical, find a Chinese person and ask them.

The radical is 宀, which is comprised of three strokes. We then look up the radical in the radical index at the front of the dictionary, by looking under the three strokes column. Turn to the page listed next to the radical, which is where all the characters with said radical are listed. If you don't know how many strokes the radical is composed of, then you'll have to search for it manually, looking at the list of radicals.

Count the remaining strokes, not including the radical – in the case of 家, there are seven strokes. Looking under number seven, we see all the characters with the 宀 radical that have seven strokes. We can then find 家 on this list, and the page number for the dictionary headword will be located next to the character. Turning to the page, we learn that the character is pronounced *jiā*, and it means 'home'.

Not a small amount of blood, sweat, and tears later, you have finished your task. Now, don't forget the character, or you'll have to look it up again. A word of warning: you will probably forget it.

Simplified characters

History shows that writing evolves from the complex to the simple. During the 1950s, the Chinese government decided to simplify the characters by reducing the number of strokes in a number of different characters and radicals. For example, the originally nine-stroke character for 'horse', *mǎ* 馬, was reduced to a three stroke character: 马.

A second round of simplifications was proposed in the 1970s, but never put into practice. These simplified characters are today used across mainland China and Singapore. Traditional characters are still used in Hong Kong, Macau and Taiwan.

The simplifications were made according to various different principles. For some characters, entire parts were simply removed. For example *guǎng* 廣, 'vast', became 广.

For other characters, the basic shape of the original was preserved, such as *fēi* 飛, 'to fly', becoming 飞; or *guī* 龜, 'turtle', becoming 龟. Another method of simplification was to adopt the unofficial shorthand for certain characters that people had been using for centuries just to save time. Good examples of this are the characters for yin and yang, the opposing energies of the universe. *Yīn* 陰 becomes 阴, and *yáng* 陽 becomes 阳.

Traditional Chinese is written vertically from top to bottom of a page, starting from the right. Simplified Chinese is written horizontally, from left to right.

> **DID YOU KNOW?**
> The five most frequently used characters in the Chinese language are:
> *de* 的: a possessive particle
> *yī* 一: meaning 'one', or 'a/an'
> *shì* 是: a verb meaning 'yes', or 'to be'
> *le* 了: a particle that can mean a lot of things – from marking the past tense to adding emphasis to a sentence
> *wǒ* 我: 'I', 'me', 'myself'
> If you can read these five characters, then you can read about 10 per cent of most simple Chinese texts.

Deconstructing a Chinese character

Mèng 梦 11 strokes, radical = 夕

As it is written today in simplified Chinese, the character *mèng* 梦, meaning **dream**, shares very little in common with its traditional form, 夢. The earliest oracle bone character for **dream** was composed of two parts – a sleeping person, waving their arms as if having a bad dream, and a bed. In the modern traditional script, the character is made up of eyebrows, eyes, and the *xī* 夕 radical, indicating 'evening', at the bottom. This radical is the only part that remains the same in its simplified form. *Zhōugōng Jiěmèng* 《周公解梦》, an ancient Chinese text used to decipher the meanings behind dreams, is still very popular today. It is attributed to the Duke of Zhou, who lived in the 11th century BC.

> ### *huángliáng mèng* 黄粱梦
> Literally 'millet dream', this literary allusion is the Chinese way of referring to a 'pipe dream'. The story goes that a poor scholar met a travelling priest at a small roadside inn. The scholar complained to the priest of his misfortune and poverty, after which the priest gave him a pillow and told him to rest his head on it. The scholar did so, and fell fast asleep, just as the innkeeper began cooking millet downstairs. The scholar dreamed that he had become fabulously wealthy, living an easy life of fame and riches. After what seemed like years in the dream world, he was awoken, and discovered that it was all a dream – and that the innkeeper had yet to finish boiling the millet. The allusion *huángliáng mèng* is today used to describe someone's unrealistic dreams. While it would do us well to heed this story and keep our feet planted on terra firma, sometimes dreams can come true, or as the Chinese say, *mèngxiǎng chéngzhēn* 梦想成真.

DID YOU KNOW?

It's said that in order to teach his ministers Chinese calligraphy, Emperor Wu of Liang (464–549 AD) asked a court official to compose a 1,000 character text with 1,000 different characters. The official completed the task in only one night, but his hair turned white in the process. The resulting text, known as the *Thousand Character Classic* (*Qiānzìwén*《千字文》) is comprised of 250 sentences, each with four characters. The classic has for centuries been used as a primer for teaching Chinese characters to children.

How many characters do you need to know?

In Chinese, each character represents a syllable, and not necessarily a word in itself. All told, there are probably around 80,000 Chinese characters. Many of these are variants of existing characters, or obsolete characters, so the number you need to learn is much lower. All students of Chinese want to know how many characters they need to memorize before they can start reading Chinese. There's no single answer, but you'll need between 3,000 to 4,000 characters to be able to read a newspaper, and more to read novels. If you learn five characters a day, every day, then it will only take a breezy two years before you know enough to start reading a newspaper! It is estimated that literate, well-educated Chinese people can recognize between 6,000 and 8,000 characters.

Taoist talismans

The Chinese religion of Taoism uses magical talismans that are highly stylized variants of Chinese characters, known as *fúlù* 符箓, or simply *fú* 符. These are drawn by Taoist priests on special yellow paper, and hung around the house to ward off evil and bring good luck. They can even be carried on the person, some offering protection against tigers and wolves whilst one roams the wilderness. Taoists claim that the fu characters are the writing of the Gods themselves.

A Taoist talisman, used to protect against evil spirits

The evolution of Chinese characters

Just as Chinese characters were not the invention of any one man, they didn't lurch from one particular style of script to the next in clearly discernible phases – the evolution of the Chinese script has been a gradual, overlapping process. The following are a variety of scripts that have been used in China, dating from over a thousand years BC to the present day.

1   Oracle bone script (*jiǎgǔwén* 甲骨文): the Oracle bone script was used during the Shang Dynasty (1600–1046 BC), mostly inscribed on tortoise shells and ox bones, used for divination purposes.

2   Bronze script (*jīnwén* 金文): the Bronze script is a term that describes a number of script styles used during the Zhou Dynasty (1045–256 BC). True to its name, most examples of Bronze script survive as inscriptions on bronze artefacts, such as bells and cauldrons.

3&4 Seal script (*zhuànshū* 篆书): the script evolved in the state of Qin during the Eastern Zhou Dynasty. It was later standardized and adopted as the national script for all of China during the Qin Dynasty (221–206 BC). It is divided into: Large Seal Script (*dàzhuàn* 大篆), used during the Zhou Dynasty; and Small Seal Script (*xiǎozhuàn* 小篆), used during the Qin Dynasty.

5 Clerical script (*lìshū* 隶书): the Clerical script first appeared during the Han dynasty (206 BC–220 AD). This is the script that students of calligraphy begin by learning.

6 Regular script (*kǎishū* 楷书): the Regular script is the newest of China's script styles, although it originated some 1,800 years ago in the third century AD. It is the script that most regular computer fonts are modelled after.

7 Running script (*xíngshū* 行书): the Running script has been used for handwritten Chinese since the Han dynasty.

8 The Grass script (*cǎoshū* 草书): this is the Chinese equivalent of shorthand and has been used since the Han dynasty. Because of its nature as a fast, easy-to-write shorthand, it can be practically illegible to the untrained eye, and can resemble chicken scratch or cobwebs. One of the hardest scripts to master in Chinese calligraphy. The character *cǎo* 草 can also be translated as 'rough' or 'sloppy'.

9 Simplified script (*jiǎntǐzì* 简体字): the Simplified script has been used in the People's Republic since 1956.

PREFACE TO THE ORCHID PAVILION COLLECTION (《*Lántíngxù*》 兰亭序)

In ancient times, Chinese scholars enjoyed the simpler of life's pleasures. They would lounge about in carefully sculpted gardens, whiling away the hours composing poetry and drinking wine. Wang Xizhi, the famed 'calligraphy sage' of the Jin Dynasty, compiled an anthology of poetry composed by his guests on one such day. The preface to this collection, known as the Orchid Pavilion Preface, is probably the most treasured example of Chinese calligraphy to have ever been penned. The poems are meditations on the fleeting nature of life, and the Preface reflects this in its gentle yet richly emotive brush strokes. Written in Running script, the Preface is used as a model of excellence for all budding calligraphers to imitate and study, and has been prized by successive Emperors of China for centuries.

The four treasures of the Chinese study

The four treasures of the Chinese study (*wénfáng sìbǎo* 文房四宝) are the tools of the trade for the Chinese scholar. Each of the 'treasures' have long artistic traditions, and fine examples are highly prized by collectors.

Writing brush

Chinese writing brushes are used for traditional calligraphy and in Chinese painting. They are usually made from animal hair. Many different kinds of animal hair can be used, although they are mostly

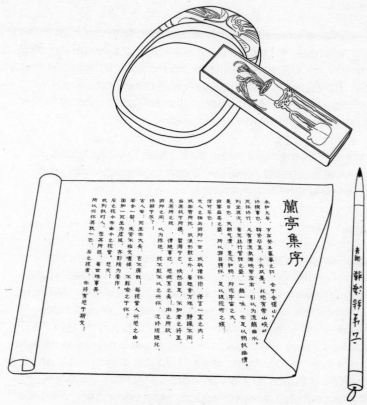

The four treasures: ink, ink stone, paper and brush

made from goat or weasel hair. Goat hair is more durable, but weasel hair brushes, known as 'wolf hair' brushes in Chinese, are prized for having a stronger tip. The material of the brush handle, usually bamboo, is not as important as the hair in the tip. They come in all kinds of sizes, from tiny, pinpoint brushes used for fine detail to huge brushes that can only be wielded with both hands. The best brushes are said to come from Huzhou, a municipal district in Zhejiang province, and are known as *Húbǐ* 湖笔.

Ink stick

Ink sticks are, in essence, solid lumps of soot. To get ink from the solid stick, you must first rub it against an ink slab to generate ink powder; secondly, water is added to the ink powder to form the ink. Although this is harder work than simply using pre-mixed bottled ink, this method allows you to easily adjust the density of the ink by adding more water or ink powder as necessary.

The ink sticks which are held in the highest regard are known as *Huīmò* 徽墨, literally 'Anhui Ink'. They are still produced today in Shexian county of Anhui province.

Paper

Paper is considered to be one of China's Four Great Inventions (the other three are the compass, gunpowder, and movable type printing). Before the invention of paper, Chinese was written on silk, bamboo strips, or carved into wood. The process of pulp paper-making was invented by imperial eunuch Cai Lun in the Han dynasty (206 BC–220 AD). Historically, the most valuable paper was made in Jingxian county in Anhui province. This paper is known as Xuan paper (*Xuānzhǐ* 宣纸) and is renowned for its soft texture and moth-resistant quality. Chinese calligraphy paper (sometimes called rice paper) is much thinner than the paper we normally use when writing with a pen.

Inkstone

The inkstone is a slab of stone with a depression in which the ink is ground and then mixed with water. While its use is simple, by the Qing dynasty ink slabs became works of art in themselves. Most inkstones are made from stone, but other materials such as pottery or jade can also used.

SCRIPTS AROUND CHINA

Some of China's ethnic groups have their own writing systems. While a number of these use alphabets, such as Tibetan and Mongolian, a few use characters that also evolved from early pictographs, such as the Dongba script of the Naxi people in Yunnan province and the Shui Script of the Sui people in Guizhou province. These pictographic scripts are not in common use today, having been all but replaced by Chinese characters.

Chapter 6: Grammar
语法
yǔfǎ

Grammar

语法
yǔfǎ

> *In writing, words become sentences, sentences combine to form chapters, and paragraphs accumulate into literary works. The splendour of a literary work is dependent on flawless chapters; the beauty of a chapter comes from blemish-free sentences, and the clarity of a sentence relies on the proper use of words.*
>
> *Liu Xie*

At the end of the nineteenth century, China endured a rude awakening to the modern world. After suffering embarrassing defeats at the hands of the imperial powers, China's intellectuals sought to discover the reasons behind their country's failures. Ma Jianchong (1844–1900), a scholar and patriot of the late Qing dynasty, believed that China's backwardness could be attributed to the very nature of its language. Indeed, as early as the eighteenth century, Western linguists had been criticizing Chinese for its 'lack of structure', seeing it as a 'primitive' language.

Perhaps influenced by Western critics, Chinese scholars introduced reforms to the written language to try and make it more logical. As an example, different characters for 'he' (tā 他), 'she' (tā 她), and 'it' (tā 它) were introduced, giving Chinese the illusion of gender distinction that it had never before possessed. These replaced the formerly universal pronoun tā 他'. To this day, Chinese people still confuse 'he' and 'she' in English.

At that time, unlike in Western countries, the rules governing Chinese grammar were not taught in its schools. One learned good Chinese by studying forms of classical literature. For Ma, China's accumulated wisdom was getting lost in its language. In an attempt to remedy the situation, Ma went on to write the first systematic treatise on Chinese grammar, and the modern study of Chinese grammar was born. At the time, Ma was criticized for forcing his interpretation of Chinese grammar onto a Western framework, as many believed Chinese to have no grammar in the traditional sense. It's worth pointing out that the Chinese for grammar, *yǔfǎ* 语法, is simply a translation of the Western word: in China, 'grammar' itself is something of a foreign concept.

By the early twentieth century, linguists had mostly dispelled the myth that there were such things as 'primitive' languages. The fallacy that 'Chinese has no grammar' still remains, however. A number of Chinese people, no doubt tormented by years of ineffectual English-language tuition, like to say that their language is grammar-free, and all the better for it. Students of Chinese will often make the same claim, a way of rationalizing their choice of subject in the face of perhaps easier foreign languages. In fact, Chinese has a lot of grammar: it's just markedly different from that of English. Chinese grammar is a bit like the highly-strategic game of Go. It looks incredibly simple from the outside, with its uniform black and white pieces, but once you have an understanding of how it works, it's easy to get lost in its remarkable complexity. When people claim that Chinese has no grammar, it's likely they just mean that it's not inflected for case, person, or tense.

Literary Chinese and the rise of the vernacular

Historically, Chinese was written in what was known as *wényánwén* 文言文, literary Chinese, a form of the language that was based on ancient grammar and vocabulary. This was used in almost all correspondence and writing until the beginning of the early twentieth century. It is still occasionally used on formal occasions today, whether in speeches or inscribed on commemorative plaques.

Command of literary Chinese is to some degree a symbol of social status. Literary Chinese has a heavily abbreviated style, and is usually awash with obscure literary references. This makes it hard for modern Chinese people to understand without formal training.

In the first decades of the twentieth century, intellectuals decided that the written language should more accurately reflect the lives of ordinary people, and more works were written in the vernacular language, known as *báihuà* 白话.

> **BÀNWÉN BÙBÁI** 半文不白
> This phrase literally means 'half literary, not vernacular', and refers to a confused linguistic style that uses partly literary, partly modern grammatical constructions. It is often used to criticize overly ornate or pretentious writing.

Today's spoken Chinese features plenty of abbreviations and reduced forms that are likely the influence of the terse style of classical Chinese. Examples of these are:

- *Wénhuà Dà Gémìng* 文化大革命, the 'Cultural Revolution', becomes simply *Wéngé* 文革
- *kōngqì tiáojiéqì* 空气调节器, 'air conditioning unit', becomes *kōngtiáo* 空调

The names of most universities in China can be reduced in this way, such as:

- *Běijīng Dàxué* 北京大学, 'Beijing University' becomes *Běi Dà*北大
- *Sìchuān Dàxué* 四川大学, 'Sichuan University' becomes *Chuān Dà* 川大

Overview of Chinese grammar

What follows is not an exhaustive or definitive account of Chinese grammar. The function of this overview is not to serve as a replacement for a text book or other form of instruction. That is beyond the scope of this book, and at any rate the subject has already been approached in greater detail, and with doubtless more wit and precision than can be accomplished here. The following is merely an introduction to a few issues concerning Chinese grammar that is intended to give the reader a very general idea of how the language works.

Characters and words

A single Chinese character often has a meaning of its own. The character *mǎ* 马 means 'a beast with four legs that can be ridden' – a horse. *Jiàn* 剑 means 'a sharp-edged weapon used in ancient China' – a sword. Sometimes however, two characters have to be used together before they can have meaning: *pútao* 葡萄 means 'grape'. If you were to just say the first character, *pú* 葡, it would have no meaning. 'Words' each have their own meaning, so *mǎ* 马 is a word, and *pútao* 葡萄 is a word. *Pú* 葡 is just a character because by itself it is meaningless, being no more meaningful than the first part of 'grape' in English – **gra**. Chinese is not, as some suggest, a monosyllabic language.

Word order

The word order of Chinese is usually classified as being of the Subject-Verb-Object type, as in English. For example, we would say 'John is a teacher'. In this case, the Chinese word order is the same: *Yuēhàn shì lǎoshī* 约翰是老师, literally 'John is [a] teacher'. In most cases, verbs and nouns are modified by what comes before them. As such, adjectives come before nouns, for example, *lánsè de qúnzi* 蓝色的裙子, 'a blue dress'.

Chinese word order is most certainly not always the same as in English. Question words in English normally occur at the start of the sentence – 'Who are you?' – for example. In Chinese, the question word is placed in the same position as the word it replaces. The question 'Who are you?' is rendered *nǐ shì shéi?* 你是谁?', literally 'you are who?'.

It is perhaps more helpful to think of Chinese sentences as divided into two parts: the 'topic', or what the sentence is about, and the rest of the sentence, or the 'comment'. Although some sentences don't have topics, if they do, it always comes first. It can sometimes be identified by a pause that separates topic from comment.

- *Zhè běn shū nǐ kàn guò ma?* 这本书你看过吗？ – 'Have you read this book?'

Here the topic is the 'book', which comes first – *zhè běn shū* 这本书, 'this book'.

- *Zhōngwén bù hǎo xué* 中文不好学 – 'Chinese isn't easy'

Here the topic is 'Chinese', *Zhōngwén* 中文.

> **yǎowén jiáozì** 咬文嚼字
> Literally meaning 'to bite words and chew on characters', this phrase means 'to nit-pick about words'.

Noun, adjective, or verb?

If we take a Chinese sentence, let's say '*gǒu yǎo rén* 狗咬人', 'dog bites man', and explain that *gǒu* 狗, 'dog', is the subject, *yǎo* 咬, 'to bite', is the verb, and *rén* 人, 'man', is the object, then we have managed to successfully convey the meaning of the sentence. We have not however gone very far into understanding how Chinese really works as a language, as we are merely explaining it in Western linguistic terms. In fact, it is a feature of Chinese words that they often serve multiple purposes. In many cases the noun is not distinguished from the verb, and the same word can be an adjective or adverb.

The character '*fù* 富' for example can mean 'rich', 'riches', or 'to make rich' – it can be an adjective, noun, or verb, all depending on the context. Similarly, the word '*hǎo* 好' can mean 'good', 'goodness', or 'to be good'. This may seem confusing at first, but the position of the word in the sentence makes it very easy to understand what its usage is: *wǒ hěn hǎo* 我很好 means 'I am fine'. In contrast, when used adjectivally it precedes the noun it modifies: *hǎo rén* 好人, means 'good person'.

HELPFUL HINT

Verbs in Chinese are all negated with the word *bù* 不, 'not', which is placed before the verb. For example:

wǒ bú yào xué yǔfǎ 我不要学语法 – 'I don't want to learn grammar'

chòudòufu bù hǎochī 臭豆腐不好吃不好 – 'stinky tofu doesn't taste good'

wǒ bú huì shuō zhōngwén 我不会说中文 – 'I can't speak Chinese'

The exception to this rule is the verb *yǒu* 有, 'to have'. It is negated by the character *méi* 没. For example:

wǒ méiyǒu bànfǎ 我没有办法 – 'there's nothing I can do'

wǒ méiyǒu qián 我没有钱 – 'I have no money'

Measure words *liàngcí* 量词

Chinese nouns do not have different plural and singular forms.
For example, 'person' and 'people' are both '*rén*', '人'. To convey
quantity, nouns are instead qualified by measure words. That is
to say, Chinese nouns are like mass nouns in English. Think of the
English word 'rice'. We say 'a grain of rice', 'a bowl of rice', or 'a sack of
rice'. We cannot just stroll into a Chinese restaurant and say 'three
rice, please'. All Chinese nouns operate in this way. 'One person' is
yī gè rén 一个人, 'three people' is *sān gè rén* 三个人. The measure
word here is ***gè*** 个, which is the most common of Chinese measure
words and is a useful catch-all substitute if you have forgotten the
right one for the noun at hand.

Measure words have to be learned along with the nouns that
they quantify. Fortunately there aren't too many in common usage,
and you can always use ***ge*** in a pinch. Some basic measure words:

tiáo 条 is the measure word for long, narrow things, such as snakes,
and roads

- *yī tiáo shé* 一条蛇 – 'one snake'
- *liǎng tiáo lù* 两条路 – 'two roads'

zhāng 张 is the measure word for long, flat things, like tables, and
sheets of paper. It can also be used for tickets

- *yī zhāng piào* 一张票 – 'one ticket'

- *liǎng zhāng zhuōzi* 两张桌子 – 'two tables'

bǎ 把 is the measure word for things with handles, such as umbrellas, knives, and swords

- *yī bǎ sǎn* 一把伞 – 'one umbrella'

- *liǎng bǎ jiàn* 两把剑 – 'two swords'

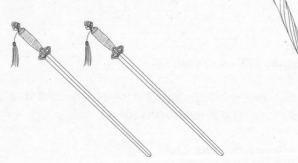

liàng 辆 is the measure word for vehicles, such as bicycles, cars, and trains

- *yī liàng zìxíngchē* 一辆自行车 – 'one bicycle'
- *liǎng liàng chē* 两辆车 – 'two cars'

zuò 座 is the measure word for large, solid objects such as buildings and mountains

- **yī zuò dàlóu** 一座大楼 – 'one building'

- **liǎng zuò shān** 两座山 – 'two mountains'

gè 个, the general classifier, can be used for a wide variety of nouns

- **yī gè rén** 一个人 – 'one person'
- **yī gè jīdàn** 一个鸡蛋 – 'one egg'
- **yī gè píngguǒ** 一个苹果 – 'one apple'

As an example of the complexity involved in learning measure words, we can look at the different measure words used for referring to people:

For most non-specific or general uses, **gè** 个 is used.

- **yī gè nánhái** 一个男孩 – 'one boy'
- **yī gè nóngmín** 一个农民 – 'one farmer'
- **yī gè shìbīng** 一个士兵 – 'one soldier'

However, in certain circumstances the politer **wèi** 位 is called for:

- *yī wèi lǎoshī* 一位老师 – 'one teacher'
- *yī wèi kèrén* 一位客人 – 'one guest'
- *yī wèi dàibiǎo* 一位代表 – 'one delegate'

The measure word **tiáo** 条 can also be used in certain situations, for example when referring to brave or heroic persons:

- *yī tiáo hǎohàn* 一条好汉 – 'one brave man'

> **HELPFUL HINT**
> Chinese personal pronouns are pluralized by adding the suffix *men* 们
>
> *wǒ* 我 is 'I', *wǒmen* 我们 is 'we'
> *nǐ* 你 is 'you', *nǐmen* 你们 is 'you' (plural)
> *tā* 他 is 'he', *tāmen* 他们 is 'them'
>
> Sometimes, *zánmen* 咱们 is used instead of *wǒmen* 我们 for expressing 'we'. *Zánmen* 咱们 includes the listener in the action. It is generally used in North China. When speaking to someone with whom you are not familiar, or someone of higher social status such as your teacher or boss, it is polite to use the pronoun *nín* 您, 'you'. This is simply a more formal way of saying 'you'. It is also impolite to use the formal *nín* 您 with someone close to you.

Past, present, or future?

Chinese verbs do not conjugate. This is a fact that can cause confusion and relief in equal measure. The English 'am', 'are', 'is', 'was', 'were', etc., can all be translated in Chinese as *shì* 是. This isn't to say that the Chinese language has no means of conveying a sense of time; only that students of Chinese don't need to worry too much about past or future constructions. This is because tense is generally indicated by context. The phrase *tāmen zài zhèr* 他们在这儿, literally 'they in here', could be interpreted as either 'they are here', or 'they were here'. Usually, the time will be made clear either by the context, or from the presence of a time expression such as today (*jīntiān* 今天) or tomorrow (*míngtiān* 明天). This is why people say Chinese has 'aspect' and not tense. That is to say, a sense of time is not conveyed by different forms of a verb, i.e. 'go' and 'went', in the case of the past tense, but by other particles that serve to indicate completion.

The past tense is commonly marked by the particle *le* 了, which indicates that an action has already been completed. For example:

- *tā qù le* 他去了 – he's gone

The future tense is marked with the modal *hui* 会, which indicates that the action will be done. For example:

- *wǒ huì qù* 我会去 – I'll go

The present tense is marked with *zài* 在, which indicates that the action is currently taking place. For example:

- *wǒ zài kànshū* 我在看书 – I'm reading

The present continuous is marked with the particle *zhe* 着, which indicates that the action is in progress or that the results of the action are continuing. For example:

- *tāmen zhèng tánzhe huà ne* 他们正谈着话呢 – they're in the middle of a conversation

The many uses of le 了

The easy-to-write and easy-to-remember particle, le 了, is often called a Chinese 'grammarian's delight'. Unfortunately, this is just another way of saying that its usage is complicated and difficult to explain. As we have seen, it can be used as a past tense marker, but it can also be used to intensify whatever comes before it, as an imperative, or to signify that a change has occurred – for example 'Xiàyǔ le! 下雨了!', 'It's started raining!'

The le 了 particle is mainly used to indicate a completed action. For example:

- tā zǒu le 他走了 – 'he has gone'

Le 了 can also be used as an imperative, that is, a command which is issued by the subject. For example:

- Bié jìnlái le! 别进来了! – 'Don't come in!'

Here, le is used in conjunction with bié ('don't') to form an imperative.

When pronounced liǎo, 了 can be used to indicate the subject's capability to do something. For example:

- wǒ shízài chī bù liǎo le 我实在吃不了了 – 'I cannot possibly eat any more'

Notice that this sentence contains two instances of the character 了, paired side-by-side. We can work out that the first '了' is pronounced liǎo given its placement – this is because le le doesn't make any sense. The liǎo here serves to indicate the capability of eating any further. The final le merely serves to add emphasis, stressing that the speaker really couldn't have another bite.

What's more, the character 了 can also be used as a verb, in which case it is pronounced *liǎo*, and can mean 'to finish' or 'to understand'.

Structural particles: the three *de* particles

Chinese has three structural particles that are all pronounced *de*, and routinely confused by native speakers as well as students of the language:

- ***de*** 的 is the possessive particle, and usually comes in between an adjective and a noun, for example: *hěn gāo de rén* 很高的人 'very tall person'. This particle is used instead of a genitive case.
- ***de*** 得 is the particle of degree, and usually comes between a verb and adjective, for example: *pǎo de kuài* 跑得快 'run fast'.
- ***de*** 地 is the adverbial particle, and usually comes between an adverb and a verb, for example: *mànmàn de dǎkāi* 慢慢地打开 'open slowly'.

The confusion is understandable, because before the twentieth century all three uses were marked with the same character: *de* 的.

Sentence final particles

Chinese makes use of a variety of sentence final particles. These particles are attached to the end of a sentence, and modify what comes before them.

Some of the most common particles are:

ma 吗
This is the question particle; this indicates that a question is being asked. It is generally used for questions with yes or no answers. For example:

- *Shì ma* 是吗？ 'Is that so?'
- *Nǐ yě qù ma* 你也去吗？ 'Are you going too?'

ne 呢

The ending particle *ne* 呢 acts as a question marker, but only when the context is already known. It's similar to saying 'How about...?' in English. A common use of *ne* is when you wish to repeat a question that has just been asked for another subject. Simply add *ne* to the end of the noun or pronoun. For example:

- *Wǒ jiào Xīméng, nǐ ne?* 我叫西蒙，你呢？ 'I'm called Simon. And you?'
- *Bùlái'ēn shì Yīngguórén, tā ne?* 布莱恩是英国人，他呢？ 'Brian is British. What about him?'

ba 吧

This is the suggestion particle; this indicates that a suggestion is being made, much like the English '...OK?'. For example:

- *Wǒmen qù kàn diànyǐng ba.* 我们去看电影吧 'Let's go see a film, OK?'

> **HELPFUL HINT**
> One of the simplest ways of making a question is to repeat the positive and negative forms of the verb:
> *Nǐ xǐhuān bù xǐhuān?* 你喜欢不喜欢？ – 'Do you like it?'
> *Nǐ lèi bú lèi?* 你累不累？ – 'Are you tired?'

A note on punctuation

Before the twentieth century, Chinese had almost no punctuation. This made reading a difficult task for the untrained reader, as one couldn't tell when one sentence would end and another would begin just by looking for the punctuation marks.

The first Chinese book to use modern punctuation was published in 1919. Modern Chinese punctuation is, on the whole, quite similar to English punctuation, but there are some differences. Chinese marks of punctuation occupy the same space as a Chinese character, so they can appear larger than their Western equivalents.

The Chinese full stop
- The full stop in Chinese is written as a small, empty circle – '。'. It acts in the same way as in English, marking the end of a sentence.
  Wǒ ài yǔfǎ. 我愛語法。 'I love grammar.'

Enumeration comma
- The enumeration comma, '、', is known as the *dùnhào* 顿号, 'pause mark' in Chinese. It is used exclusively between items that form a list.

Book and film titles
- Book and film titles are signified with the use of full width, double angle brackets '《…》'. When embedded within the former, full width, single angle brackets '〈…〉' are used.

Ellipsis
- The Chinese ellipsis is written with six dots – '……', not the three used in English, and they occupy the same space as two characters. They should be written in the middle of the line, not along the bottom.

Final thoughts

While European languages tend to have sophisticated systems of conjugation and declension, in contrast Chinese can seem excessively simple. There is no diversity of genders, cases and declinations in the spoken Chinese language. As a result, you'd be forgiven for thinking that Chinese as a language can't possibly match the complexity of English, with its conjugating verbs and Oxford commas. Widely available translations of classical Chinese poetry, with their simplistic imagery of full, bright moons and bamboo leaves swaying in the wind, do little to dispel this impression. But the truth is that it's misleading to try and compare languages in this way. It's enough that we recognize the Chinese language as the tool most suited to reflecting the thoughts of its people – no more, no less.

Chapter 7:
Names and forms of address
姓名与称呼方式
xìngmíng yǔ
chēnghū fāngshì

Names and forms of address
姓名与称呼方式
xìngmíng yǔ chēnghū fāngshì

The Son of Heaven rewarded the meritorious with noble ranks, and bestowed family names upon them according to their places of birth.
The Chronicle of Zuo

A person's name accompanies them throughout their whole lives. It is natural then that the Chinese have attached great importance to names and the art of naming since ancient times. In China, people believe that a good name will bring you good fortune, and a bad name will leave you with nothing but a lifetime of regret. Villages around the country fight to be recognized as the true ancestral homes of famous genealogies, from the *Máo* 毛 family that produced China's 'Great Helmsman', Mao Zedong 毛泽东, to the family of one of China's most renowned strategists, Zhuge Liang 诸葛亮 (181–234 AD). It is considered a great honour to share a surname with a famous person, even if one is not even tangentially related to them.

Chinese people use five criteria to distinguish a 'good' name from a 'bad' one:

- **Easy to say** – such names as San Mao 三毛 and Hu Gua 胡瓜 fall under this category. In contrast, names that have characters that all share the third tone – Liu Jingxuan 柳景选, for example – are considered 'difficult' to say.
- **Pleasant sounding** – names such as Lin Daojing 林道静 and Zhou Xuan 周旋 are believed to sound nice when spoken in Mandarin.
- **Easy to write** – names that feature simple characters, consisting of only a few strokes, such as Ding Yisan 丁一三 and Wang Erxiao 王二小.

- **Nice to look at** – names that use characters considered to be aesthetically pleasing, such as Deng Lijun 邓丽君 and Jiang Yan 江雁.
- **Easy to remember** – usually names that conjure up a certain image, such as Xia Meng 夏梦 (Summer Dream), or Wu Tong 吴桐 (Chinese parasol tree).

If a name fails to satisfy even one of the above criteria, then it cannot be considered a 'good name'.

In modern China, most people's names consist of two to three characters. Some family names have two or more characters, but these are relatively rare. The three-character name is most traditionally broken down into the following:

- a **family name**,
- followed by the **generation name**,
- and finally the **given name**.

Family names

As befits a culture that emphasizes the importance of family, Chinese 'family names' or *xìngshì* 姓氏, come first. The first character in a Chinese name, passed down from the father's side, is the family name – the equivalent of an English surname. This is followed by the given name, of either one or two characters.

China has a wealth of family names: there are literally thousands, but you wouldn't think it by looking at any school class register, for example. Around 20 surnames alone account for a vast majority of the country's population.

It is not uncommon to find entire villages populated by people who all share the same surname. Place names reflect the predominance of certain families. A village such as *Yángjiākuàng* 杨家矿, literally 'Yang Family Mine', would historically have belonged to a certain landowning family by the name of *Yáng*.

Origins of family names

A number of Chinese surnames are taken from the names of animals, such as *Mǎ* 马 (horse), *Xióng* 熊 (bear), *Niú* 牛 (ox), *Yáng* 羊 (sheep), and *Lóng* 龙 (dragon). Some believe that this practice comes from the primitive totemic worship of such animals.

Family names can also originate from the titles of estates and lands given to lords throughout history. Examples of this would be *Wú* 吴, the name of a land bequeathed to the grandson of a favoured court official by King Wu of Zhou, *Zhōu Wǔ wáng* 周武王. Later generations of the ruling family were surnamed *Wú*. Some family names also originate from official titles, such as the two character *Sītú* 司徒, which means 'minister of education', while others refer to the position of the family's hereditary home, such as *Dōngmén* 东门, literally 'eastern gate'.

The family name Wang dates back to the sixth century AD. The Chinese character *Wáng* 王 can mean either 'king' or 'the highest official rank of nobility that an emperor may grant his subject'. Apart from those who were members of the imperial family – the *wángzú* 王族, or 'royalty' – a lot of people were granted the surname as an honour, and some even carried it falsely. The family name is not limited solely to descendants of the Chinese imperial family, but also found among the descendants of tribal leaders and the rulers of many ethnic groups.

Chinese people who share the same family name often like to claim that they are related, tracing their common heritage back centuries into the past. In reality, this is rarely true, as any major surname may in fact have a hundred or more original blood lines. China's most common surname, *Lǐ* 李, is a good example. During the Tang dynasty, this surname was granted to a number of loyal subjects who helped found the dynasty. The surname was bestowed upon them by the emperor *Lǐ Shìmín* 李世民, and of course it was a great honour to share the surname of the Emperor.

Zhāng 张 is another common Chinese family name. The Chinese character 'Zhang' is composed of the character *gōng* 弓, meaning 'bow', on the left and *cháng* 长, meaning 'long', on the right. Taken as a whole, the character looks like a man drawing a bow, ready to shoot. It is said that the surname was first taken by the grandson of the Yellow Emperor himself, who was a great inventor, counting the bow and arrow among his inventions.

> **DID YOU KNOW?**
>
> China refers to its regular civilians as *lǎobǎixìng* 老百姓, 'the old one hundred surnames'. In ancient times, this phrase was exclusively used to describe the Chinese nobility, because before the fifth century BC, only high-ranked feudal officials had surnames. After the Warring States period (475–221 BC), it came to be used as a term for the common folk. It is said that around 85 per cent of Chinese people share the most common hundred surnames.

Given names

The art of finding a good name could be considered to be a more complicated process in China than it is in the West. Whereas in English-speaking cultures parents mostly look for names that sound good, in China one must consider the meaning of the characters in the name, as well as what the characters look like. Both are equally as important as the pronunciation of the name itself. But this is not all: a good name should also take into account the customs and traditions of Chinese elemental astrology – the signs of the zodiac and the five elements – to make sure that the characters used do not make for an unlucky combination.

Given names are usually one or two characters in length. The first character of a given name was traditionally the 'generation name', or *zìbèi* 字辈.

The sequence of generation names is normally written down in the form of a generation poem (*bāncì lián* 班次联). Each successive character in the poem is used as the generation name for successive generations of the family. A well-known example is the family lineage of Confucius. The generational poem of Confucius' family is inscribed on a wall of the Confucius Temple in his home town of Qufu, modern day Shandong province. A part of the poem reads:

> '昭宪庆繁祥
> *'Zhāo xiàn qìng fán xiáng*
> 令德维垂佑'
> *Lìng dé wéi chuí yòu'*

From this we can surmise that if Kong Xiangzhen 孔祥祯 is the seventy-fifth descendant of Confucius, then Kong Lingpeng 孔令彭 is the seventy-sixth, and Kong Demao 孔德懋 is the seventy-seventh. This is because the character *lìng* 令 directly follows that of *xiáng* 祥 in the poem, and *dé* 德 follows on from *lìng* 令, thus marking successive generations of the family.

As we have seen, everyone wants to choose a good name for their children. China is a populous country, and some names are very common. Take the given name *Héng* 衡, for example. As a name, it has the meaning of 'measured' or 'balanced', and is very commonly seen throughout history. In the Eastern Han dynasty, there was a scientist known as Zhang Heng 张衡; the Tang dynasty had a poet named Yang Heng 杨衡; in the Song dynasty there was a scholar named Huang Heng 黄衡; in the Ming dynasty, there was an artist called Xia Heng 夏衡; and in the Qing dynasty there was a painter called Ma Heng 马衡.

Li Na 李娜 is an example of a very common combination of family name and given name in today's China. It is the name of a Chinese diver, as well as a star tennis player, a fencer, a recording artist and likely countless other less famous people. To avoid this repetition, some parents go to great lengths to choose odd or rare characters for their children's given names. They will search through ancient dictionaries, trying to find unusual characters that will make their children stand out, finally choosing such characters as: *yàn* 谳, 'to decide judicially'; *shèng* 晟, 'splendour'; and *bèi* 鞴, 'to saddle and bridle a horse'.

These names, while relatively unique, can cause problems for whomever they belong to. The great sinologist Zhang Taiyan 章太炎 (1869–1936) was someone who discovered the unexpected downsides to giving one's children odd names. He named all three of his daughters with ancient variants of modern characters that few but the most die-hard of Chinese linguists would recognize; variants that could not be found in dictionaries. When it came time for the girls to be married, Zhang found that no suitors came knocking. This was especially unusual as all three were considered very attractive and capable women, and their good family background goes without saying. It was some time before Zhang discovered the reason: while many eligible bachelors wished to court his daughters, they were all afraid to ask permission because they did not know how to correctly pronounce their unusual names! To resolve the issue, Zhang arranged for a banquet to be held in his home, inviting all his friends and family. During the banquet he subtly revealed the correct pronunciations of his daughters' names, and over the next few days, a wealth of suitors came to his door.

In addition, some names have meanings that are arrogant and presumptuous, and these are obviously best avoided. The names *Shìxióng* 世雄, 'worldwide hero', *Tiāncái* 天才, 'genius', and *Wénshèng* 文圣, 'literary sage', are all examples of such names. If the so-called fails to live up to their namesake, then they can all too easily become the object of ridicule.

Some Chinese names can reflect the important events of the time in which the person was born. After the Communist revolution, many Chinese given names were steeped in a heavy political flavour. In the late 1940s and early 1950s, given names such as *Jiànguó* 建国 (founding of the state), *Shènglì* 胜利 (victory), and *Jiěfàng* 解放 (liberation), were very popular. During the Cultural Revolution from the late 1960s to the 1970s, names such as *Wéngé* 文革 (cultural revolution) and *Wèibīng* 卫兵 (guardsman) were in vogue. Ever since the period of reform and opening up in the 1980s, however, names have become increasingly less politicized.

Cultural revolution-style poster. The top banner reads: 'Serve the people'.

Boys' names

Parents will normally select characters that reflect 'masculine' traits when naming their sons. These names fall into the following categories:

- Characters that are considered 'strong', such as *gāng* 钢 'steel', and *tiě* 铁, 'iron'.
- Characters that reflect ambition and drive, such as *qiánjìn* 前进, 'to advance', and *chéngcái* 成才, 'to become a talented person'.
- Characters that illustrate a desire for long life, such as *guīsuì* 龟岁, 'long-lived like a tortoise'.
- Words that reflect a desire for wealth, such as *yǒucái* 有财, 'to have riches'.
- Words that illustrate strength and power, such as *dàhǔ* 大虎, 'great tiger'.

Girls' names

As might be expected, Chinese girls' names differ from boys' names. It is common for parents to select 'feminine' characters when naming their daughters and these can be grouped into the following categories:

- Characters that have the 'female' radical – *nǚzìpáng* 女字旁. Characters such as *juān* 娟, 'graceful', *jiāo* 姣, 'pretty', and *tíng* 婷, 'dainty', are all seen to be fitting for a girl's name.
- Names of birds or flowers, such as *lán* 兰, 'orchid', and *yàn* 燕, 'swallow'.
- Names of objects associated with a woman's bedchamber, such as *huán* 环, 'bracelet', and *chāi* 钗, 'hairpin'.
- Characters associated with landscape and nature, such as *xiá* 霞, 'daybreak', and *shuāng* 霜, 'frost'.
- Characters associated with female virtues, such as *shū* 淑, 'virtuous and gentle', and *zhēn* 贞, 'chaste'.

Pet names

The naming of household pets in China does not follow any strict custom, although pet names frequently fall into one of two categories:

- Adding the prefix ā 阿, such as *āhuáng* 阿黄, and *ādōng* 阿东.
- Repeating a single character, such as *tiántián* 甜甜 (sweety), or *měiměi* 美美 (beauty).

Choosing a Chinese name

Foreign names in Chinese are usually simply transliterated. Charles Dickens, for example, is translated as *Chá'ěrsī Dígēngsī*查尔斯·狄更斯, and Shakespeare is *Shāshìbǐyà* 莎士比亚. Foreign names seem wordy and over-long in comparison to Chinese names, which are mostly just two or three syllables in length. Many foreigners who spend time in the country decide to choose a Chinese name, which can help them to make friends and do business in China – it is after all difficult for Chinese people who have not had much language training to remember a foreign name.

Methods of choosing a Chinese name:

- Direct phonetic translation. These straight transliterations, while simple, can lead to amusing and unintended meanings in Chinese. The name Sarah is often directly translated as *Shālā* 莎拉, which sounds identical to *shālā* 沙拉, 'salad', in Chinese. Similarly, the Spanish name Roberto, when directly translated, would be *Lóbotóu* 萝卜头, or literally 'radish head'. Even more unfortunate is the short name Ben, which can be read as the pinyin *bèn* 笨, or 'stupid'. While easy to remember, such names always sound distinctly 'foreign' and can mark you as an outsider.
- Highlighting a particular physical or character trait. Perhaps China's most famous foreigner, the Canadian broadcaster and

performer Mark Rowswell, has a memorable Chinese name: *Dàshān* 大山. This literally translates as 'high mountain', and can probably be explained by the Canadian's towering height.

- Phonetic translation that retains the flavour of a Chinese name. This is one of the more subtle and most difficult methods of choosing a Chinese name. The former deputy spokesperson for the US State Department, Allen Romburg, chose the name Rong Anlan 容安澜. Rong is a Chinese family name that sounds similar to the first part of his own surname, and the Chinese *ānlán* 安澜 is a word that means 'calm and unruffled', a word that also happens to sound very similar in pronunciation to the English name 'Allen'.

- Choose a completely unrelated name. Nobody says you have to choose a Chinese name that sounds like your original name. You can choose any combination of surname and given names that takes your fancy. It is best to avoid famous Chinese names like Li Xiaolong 李小龙 (Bruce Lee) or Cheng Long 成龙 (Jackie Chan). Imagine someone coming up to you and saying that their English name is Clint Eastwood. Amusing? Yes. Wise in the long term? No.

HELPFUL TIP

It's always polite to ask someone what they are called when first meeting them. Here's how to do this in Chinese:

Asking someone's name:

Qǐng wèn, wǒ gāi zěnme chēnghu nín? 请问，我该怎么称呼您？ – 'May I ask what I should call you?'

This is used not only to ask someone's name, but also to ask if they have any preferred form of address.

Qǐng wèn, zūnxìng dàmíng? 请问尊姓大名？ – 'May I ask your name?'

This is the polite way of asking for someone's name.

Nǐ jiào shénme míngzì? 你叫什么名字？ – 'What's your name?'

This is the more colloquial, less formal way of asking someone's name.

To answer, one would say:

Wǒ jiào… 我叫⋯⋯ – 'My name is…'

Chengyu idioms and names

There are several set phrases in the Chinese language that revolve around the use of the family names *Zhāng* and *Lǐ* as 'everyman' names, not unlike 'Smith' in English.

- *Zhāngguān Lǐdài* 张冠李戴. Literally 'put Zhang's hat on Li's head', this means either 'attributing something to the wrong person', or 'to confuse one thing with another'.
- *Zhāngjiā cháng Lǐjiā duǎn* 张家长李家短. Literally 'to say good things about the Zhang household and bad things about the Li household', this saying is used to refer to making idle gossip.
- *Zhāngsān Lǐsì* 张三李四. Literally 'any old Zhang or Li', this saying is equivalent to the English 'any Tom, Dick, or Harry'. Where those three given names are used to refer to anybody – because they are seen as being common – the Chinese employs the family names *Zhāng* and *Lǐ*, themselves both very common in China.

> **DID YOU KNOW?**
> The top five surnames in mainland China (by population) are:
>
> 1. *Lǐ* 李
> 2. *Wáng* 王
> 3. *Zhāng* 张
> 4. *Liú* 刘
> 5. *Chén* 陈

Historical courtesy names

In addition to their given names, Chinese people often used to take on a courtesy, or style name, to be used later in life. There were two common forms of courtesy name, the *zì* 字 and *hào* 号. After turning 20, the *zì* 字 was assigned as a signifier of adulthood and respect. They were primarily used by men. A style name could be given by one's parents, a teacher, or self-chosen. Ever since the May Fourth Movement in 1919, the practice of using style names has gradually died out.

Style names were chosen specifically to share similarities with one's given name – so much so that a clever person could guess your given name just from hearing your style name. Zhuge Liang 诸葛亮, the famous military strategist during the Three Kingdoms period, had the style name Kong Ming 孔明. His given name, *liàng* 亮, means 'light', and is synonymous with the *míng* 明, 'bright', in his style name.

Names that cannot be said

The Emperors of ancient China, as the 'sons of heaven', were naturally seen to be superior to all they ruled over. This meant that their given names were taboo, and could not be spoken or written down.

This practice began during the Qin dynasty and persisted until the fall of Imperial China in the early twentieth century. Different emperors enforced this rule to different degrees; some would simply disallow subjects from using their given name to address them directly, others would forbid people from naming their children with the same name. The furthest extreme would be to ban all characters with the same pronunciation as their given name in both speech and writing.

Qín Shǐ Huáng 秦始皇, the first emperor of the Qin dynasty, was the first to use the imperial taboo. His father was named *Chǔ* 楚, and so

Qín Shǐ Huáng re-named the entire kingdom of *Chǔ* to *Jīng* 荆 to avoid the usage of his father's given name. Han emperor *Huìdì* 惠帝 had the given name of *Yíng* 盈, which means 'filled'. He decreed that every time this character was written, it should instead be changed to the character *mǎn* 满, which shares the same meaning. Sometimes an emperor would make it easier for his subjects by changing his own name to a less common character. Cao Huang 曹璜 (246–302), fifth emperor of the Kingdom of Cao Wei (*Cáo Wèi* 曹魏) during the Three Kingdoms Period, changed his name to Cao Huan 曹奂 after ascending the throne. This avoided the taboo of his given name *Huang*, which would also have tabooed other similar sounding words such as 'yellow' (*huáng* 黄) and 'emperor' (*huáng* 皇). By the early twentieth century, imperial China came to an end and this practice was discontinued.

Terms of address

In the family

Within the family, Chinese terms of address can get quite complicated. Whereas in English we simply have 'aunts and uncles' and 'grandmothers and grandfathers', the Chinese language has different words for the relatives on the mother's and father's side. This makes it all too easy to get one's generations, and even sides of the family, completely mixed up. For those Chinese people who happen to have large extended families, the extremely specific terms of address found in the Chinese language can prove to be a real headache.

On the mother's side: *lǎolao* 姥姥, 'maternal grandmother'; *lǎoyé* 姥爷, 'maternal grandfather'; *jiùjiu* 舅舅, 'maternal uncle'; *jiùmā* 舅妈, 'wife of mother's brother'; *āyí* 阿姨, 'maternal aunt'; *yífù* 姨父, 'husband of mother's sister'.

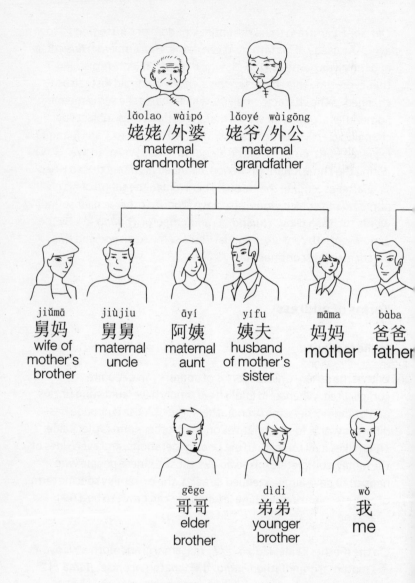

lǎolao / wàipó
姥姥 / 外婆
maternal grandmother

lǎoyé / wàigōng
姥爷 / 外公
maternal grandfather

jiǔmā
舅妈
wife of mother's brother

jiùjiu
舅舅
maternal uncle

āyí
阿姨
maternal aunt

yífu
姨夫
husband of mother's sister

māma
妈妈
mother

bàba
爸爸
father

gēge
哥哥
elder brother

dìdi
弟弟
younger brother

wǒ
我
me

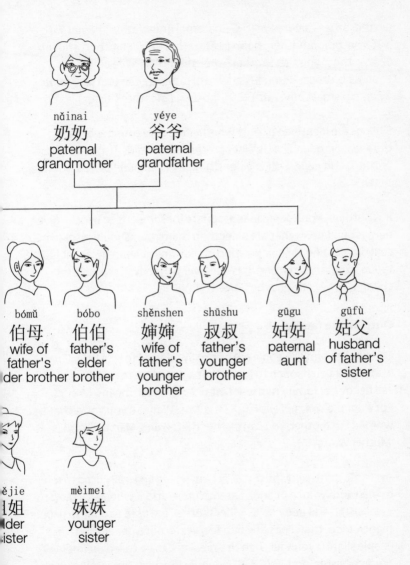

nǎinai
奶奶
paternal
grandmother

yéye
爷爷
paternal
grandfather

bómǔ
伯母
wife of
father's
elder brother

bóbo
伯伯
father's
elder
brother

shěnshen
婶婶
wife of
father's
younger
brother

shūshu
叔叔
father's
younger
brother

gūgu
姑姑
paternal
aunt

gūfù
姑父
husband
of father's
sister

ějie
姐
der
sister

mèimei
妹妹
younger
sister

Family tree and terms of address

On the father's side: *yéye* 爷爷, 'paternal grandfather'; *nǎinai* 奶奶, 'paternal grandmother'; *bóbo* 伯伯, 'father's elder brother'; *shūshu* 叔叔 'father's younger brother'; *shěnshen* 婶婶, 'wife of father's younger brother'; *bómǔ* 伯母, 'wife of father's elder brother', *gūgu* 姑姑, 'paternal aunt'; *gūfù* 姑父, 'husband of father's sister'.

Siblings are identified by age, whether they are younger or older than the speaker: *gēge* 哥哥 is 'elder brother', while *dìdi* 弟弟 is 'younger brother'; and *jiějie* 姐姐 is 'elder sister', while *mèimei* 妹妹 is 'younger sister'.

It is normally considered inappropriate for someone to use the given names of relatives that are older than them: they should instead be called according to their position in the family hierarchy, and it is a big taboo to get these wrong. It is however perfectly acceptable for children to be called by their given names.

Outside the family

Outside the family, people are normally referred to by a title. For example, if you happen to know that a woman is married, you can call her by her **family name + *Tàitai*** 太太, which means 'Mrs. ...'. For example, *Wáng Tàitai* 王太太 is 'Mrs. Wang'. If you know that a woman is a mother, you can call her that: *Wáng Māma* 王妈妈 is 'Mother Wang'.

Āyí 阿姨, 'aunt', and *shūshu* 叔叔, 'uncle', are generally used to refer to men and women of one's parents' generation, whereas *jiějie* 姐姐, 'elder sister' and *gēge* 哥哥, 'older brother' are used to refer to people slightly older than oneself – by a few years, not a generation. People slightly younger than the speaker can be called *mèimei* 妹妹, 'younger sister', and *dìdi* 弟弟, 'younger brother'. This is not a way of claiming some long-lost familial relationship, but is merely a friendly way of calling out to someone.

Depending on their age and the age of the speaker, it is common for people to be called either *lǎo* 老, 'old' or *xiǎo* 小, 'young', followed by their family name, for example *Lǎo Zhāng* 老张, 'old Zhang', or *Xiǎo Wáng* 小王, 'Young Wang'. Old people are venerated in Chinese culture, so old is not disrespectful in any way – unless used to describe a woman who is actually still young!

Great offence can be caused by calling a woman *āyí* (auntie) instead of *jiě* (sister); and likewise by calling someone *lǎo* (old) instead of *xiǎo* (young). A good tactic is to listen out for what other people say, and simply copy that – although never forget that your own age is an important factor in what you call other people. Friends tend to call each other by name, and if someone's name consists of only two characters, they will usually be called by both their family name and given name.

In China, people are very much defined by what they do. Their job title becomes an appellation: a 'teacher' is *lǎoshī* 老师 (*Chén Lǎoshī* 陈老师, 'Teacher Chen'), and a chief editor would be *zhǔbiān* 主编 (*Lǐ Zhǔbiān* 李主编, 'Chief Editor Li').

If you are unclear, the safest way to refer to someone is by using the polite *xiānshēng* 先生 (Mr.), and *nǚshì* 女士 (Mrs.). These can be used both together with family names: *nǐhǎo, Sūn xiānshēng* 你好, 孙先生 (hello, Mr. Sun); or without: *nǐhǎo, xiānshēng* 你好, 先生 (hello, sir).

MEETING GOVERNMENT OFFICIALS

It's important to address higher-up government officials in today's China by their appropriate rank and status. When you are introduced, you will learn their position and title, and thus how to refer to them. The more common of these are: *bùzhǎng* 部长 'department head'; *chùzhǎng* 处长, 'section chief', and *zhǔrèn* 主任, 'director'. If you are unclear, listen out for how others address them. If someone says, for example, *Xú Zhǔrèn* 徐主任, 'Director Xu', you can just follow suit.

Chapter 8:
Sayings
俗话
súhuà

Sayings

俗话
súhuà

From childhood I read many, many poems and verses, and listened to many, many proverbs. And everywhere I went, I picked up proverbs.
Jiang Zemin, former CCP General Party Secretary

To the Western mind, Chinese is a language rich in idioms. From fortune cookie wisdom – 'beware odours from unfamiliar sources' – to 'Confucius, he say…' jokes, the Chinese language is seen as a goldmine of pithy sayings and wise philosophical maxims. As with most stereotypes, there is an element of truth in this view, although it has become a little distorted along the way. After all, being an American invention, most fortune cookie 'fortunes' are complete nonsense to the average Chinese person.

The Chinese do however have a deep love and respect for their language, and most everyday conversations are peppered with idioms, proverbs, and puns. Knowing these sayings will not only help improve your communication skills but also open your eyes to the history and culture of China. Chairman Mao himself was famous for using traditional sayings in his efforts to modernize the traditional peasant-based agricultural society of the times. He likened the modernization movement to the saying '*Yúgōng yíshān* 愚公移山', the old man who was labelled as foolish for believing he could move mountains with the help of successive generations of descendants. Mao also famously mocked US imperialism by comparing it to a 'paper tiger' (*zhǐlǎohǔ* 纸老虎) – something that is fierce-looking on the outside, but very easily defeated by the gentlest poke of a finger.

China's idioms and proverbs, its collected folk wisdom, are an expression of the Chinese philosophy that the collective be placed above the individual. Collective wisdom is seen as greater than individual opinion. This philosophy was successfully borrowed by the Chinese Communist Party, and the use of idioms and sayings is still central to the thinking of China's leaders even today.

Chinese idioms and sayings, which number in the tens, if not hundreds, of thousands, are seen as a direct reflection of one's learning and cultural knowledge. Chinese people like to test themselves, and others, on their knowledge of idioms, and alongside 'How many characters do you know?', 'Can you understand Chinese idioms?' is a question often asked of foreigners in China.

It's worth pointing out the difference between popular sayings in Chinese and those in English. The majority of English proverbs have fallen into complete obscurity. Those that are still in use are mostly of the unaffected, colloquial type, such as 'a stitch in time saves nine' (it's best to solve a small problem before it becomes a larger one). The Chinese language has its share of this kind of phrase, but its sayings instead more prominently feature cultural and historical knowledge. While it's true that English also has a wealth of classical allusions, like 'sword of Damocles' and 'crossing the Rubicon', very few are standard to everyday conversation, and most are borrowed from a variety of cultures and languages. Chinese idioms and proverbs are taken from thousands of years of continuous history and literature, and distilled into set phrases that have become an integral part of the modern language.

Some of the following categories are fluid; proverbs are sometimes classified as *chéngyǔ* idioms, and allegories as proverbs, or vice-versa. The exact classification of these sayings is in many ways less important than a proper understanding of when and how to use them.

Chéngyǔ

Chéngyǔ form probably the most well-known category of Chinese saying – and the most dauntingly large. *Chéngyǔ* 成语, which in Chinese literally means 'set phrases', are fixed usage idioms, mostly four syllables in length. It's said that over 90 per cent of Chinese *chéngyǔ* are composed of four characters. This is because the Chinese language can be said to naturally form words and phrases in twos, and as a result *chéngyǔ* are sometimes mistakenly labelled 'four character idioms'. This is a little misleading, as longer *chéngyǔ* do exist, although they are in the definite minority. *Chéngyǔ* are a simple way of expressing a certain meaning that can describe a person or state of affairs, or offer up a snapshot of worldly wisdom. The majority of *chéngyǔ* idioms have been passed down from ancient times, and as such their wording is naturally different to that of modern Mandarin.

> ### *CHÉNGYǓ* DICTIONARIES
> Because of the sheer number of idioms in Chinese, *chéngyǔ* dictionaries are some of the most popular reference books in China. They are a one-stop reference for all the major Chinese idioms, which are listed in alphabetical order according to their pronunciation in pinyin. They are known as *chéngyǔ cídiǎn* 成语词典.

Chéngyǔ idioms can be divided into two distinct groups: those that are based on stories, mostly originating in the literature of ancient China, and idioms that trace their roots to the everyday speech of the common person.

Idioms of the first group are the distilled essence of a story or fable. Broadly speaking, they fall into four categories:

Ancient legends:

Jīngwèi tiānhǎi 精卫填海, which literally means 'the mythical bird, Jingwei, trying to fill the ocean with stones'. Figuratively, this idiom means 'to have dogged determination in the face of impossible odds'. It comes from the *Shānhǎijīng* 《山海经》, *Classic of Mountains and Seas*, a compilation of mythology and folk customs written in around 500 BC.

Allegories:

kèzhōu qiújiàn 刻舟求剑. This phrase literally means 'to carve a notch on the side of a boat in order to mark the point where a sword was dropped overboard'. It is a metaphor for 'an action that is rendered pointless by changing circumstances', because the boat is of course carried along by the current, leaving the notch meaningless.

Hándān xuébù 邯郸学步. The phrase 'learn how to walk in Handan' is first seen in the *Zhuāngzǐ* 《庄子》, an ancient Chinese Taoist text. There was once a youth from the state of Yan who travelled to Handan, the capital of the state of Zhao, to imitate how the people there walked. Unfortunately, not only did he not master the art of walking after the fashion of the state of Zhao, he also forgot his own way of walking. He had no choice but to crawl back home using only his hands. Thus the phrase 'learn how to walk in Handan' is used to refer to someone who imitates others badly, and loses their individuality in the process.

Historical events:

pòfǔ chénzhōu 破釜沉舟, literally 'to break the cauldrons and sink the boats'. This phrase means 'to cut off all means of retreat'. The phrase is first found in the *Records of the Grand Historian*, written in the first century BC, and refers to the defeat of the warlord Xiangyu by the first Han Emperor.

wánbì guīzhào 完璧归赵, 'returning the jade intact to Zhao'. During the Warring States Period, the king of Zhao received a very rare, very valuable piece of jade. When the king of Qin heard about this, he offered him 15 cities in exchange for the jade. Qin was a powerful kingdom, so the king of Zhao did not dare refuse, even though he knew the king of Qin could not be trusted. And so he entrusted a court official, Lin Xiangru, to deliver the jade to Qin, saying 'If the king of Qin fulfils his part of the bargain and offers 15 cities in exchange for the jade, then by all means make the exchange. But if he does not offer the cities, then you must find a way to bring the jade back to us, intact'. As soon as he set eyes on it, the king of Qin fell in love with the precious jade. He paraded it around the court, praising its peerless beauty. But he made no mention of the promised 15 cities, and Lin Xiangru soon realized that he had no intention of making the exchange at all. Lin knew he had to recover the jade, so he said to the king: 'Your grace, this jade has a small flaw in it'. Reaching out as if to point out the flaw to the king, he instead stole it away. He told the king that he could not give him the jade unless the 15 cities were exchanged for it as promised. The king laughed, and asked Lin how he was planning on escaping Qin with the jade – and his head – intact. To which Lin said, 'If the king forces my hand, I will smash the jade, along with my own head, against this pillar'. Seeing that he was serious, the king had no choice but to let him return to Zhao with the jade. Now, when something is returned intact to its owner, one can say *wánbì guīzhào* 完璧归赵, or 'returning the jade intact to Zhao'.

Chinese literature:

tiānxià wūyā yībān hēi 天下乌鸦一般黑, literally 'all crows in the world are just as black'. This idiom is a way of saying that 'evil people around the world are just as bad as one another', and comes from the Qing dynasty novel, *Dream of the Red Chamber*, *Hóng Lóu Mèng* 《红楼梦》.

sāngù máolú 三顾茅庐, 'three humble visits to a thatched cottage'. This phrase come from a famous episode in the fictional *Romance of Three Kingdoms Sānguó Yǎnyì* 《三国演义》, in which the warlord Liu Bei 刘备 recruits strategist Zhuge Liang 诸葛亮 to his cause by visiting him three times. The first two times he visits, Zhuge Liang is not at home. He decides to visit a third time, and finds Zhuge Liang asleep. Instead of waking him, Liu Bei waits for Zhuge Liang to wake naturally before making his offer. The phrase is now used to mean 'to call on someone repeatedly to take up a post'.

Chéngyǔ idioms that come from the vernacular speech of the common people are set phrases that do not come from any particular story. They are simply interesting constructions that have become part of everyday speech. They do not tend to have metaphorical or allegorical meanings, and one can usually work out their meaning just by looking at the characters. For example, *húsī luànxiǎng* 胡思乱想, 'to let one's imagination run wild' is composed of the two phrases, 'reckless thought' (*húsī* 胡思) and 'wild imaginings' (*luànxiǎng* 乱想). Similarly, the idiom *bùsān bùsì* 不三不四, literally 'neither three nor four', means 'neither one thing nor the other'.

It's important to keep in mind that *chéngyǔ* are not quotations: they are expressions that have entered everyday vocabulary through general usage. Take the following sentence, which is actually two lines of verse from the Tang poet Liu Yuxi:

Chénzhōu cèpàn qiān fān guò, bìngshù qiántóu wàn mù chūn
沉舟侧畔千帆过，病树前头万木春

By the side of a vessel sunk, a thousand sails float past; In the face of a decaying tree, thousands of trees burst with life

This phrase means 'the power of the new cannot be held back'. Such quotations are not normally used in conversation, but might instead appear in an article or other literary work. The contrast between this and the short, pithy four character *chéngyǔ* is obvious.

Usage

Chinese *chéngyǔ* idioms can be used as different parts of speech in different situations.

- As adjectives: the *chéngyǔ*, *rúhuā sìyù* 如花似玉, literally 'like flowers and jade', is used to mean 'very beautiful', and is a straightforward adjective. For example: *yī gè rúhuā sìyù de gūniang* 一个如花似玉的姑娘, 'a beautiful young girl'.
- As verbs: the *chéngyǔ*, *huàshé tiānzú* 画蛇添足, literally means 'to draw legs on a snake', and is a metaphor for overdoing something. For example: *gòule, bié huàshé tiānzú* 够了，别画蛇添足, 'that's enough, don't overdo it'.
- As nouns: the *chéngyǔ*, *jìnghuā shuǐyuè* 镜花水月, literally means 'flowers reflected in a mirror and the moon reflected in a pool', and is used as a way of referring to something illusory. For example: *tāmen zhījiān de àiqíng xiàng jìnghuā shuǐyuè* 他们之间的爱情像镜花水月, 'the love between them was like an illusion'.

CHÉNGYǓ THAT ARE BASICALLY THE SAME IN CHINESE AND ENGLISH

While most *chéngyǔ* require a literal and figurative meaning in order to be properly explained in English, some have the same literal meaning in English as they do in Chinese.

huǒshàng jiāoyóu 火上浇油, 'add fuel to the flames'

yǐ yǎn huán yǎn, yǐ yá huán yá 以眼还眼，以牙还牙, 'an eye for an eye, a tooth for a tooth'. This idiom is a foreign loan.

yǎnjiàn wéishí 眼见为实, 'seeing is believing'

jiànshù bù jiànlín 见树不见林, 'can't see the wood for the trees'

chènrè dǎtiě 趁热打铁, 'strike while the iron is hot'

Getting *chéngyǔ* wrong

Knowing the *chéngyǔ* is only half the battle. Being familiar with the story behind it is also quite necessary – as the former President of the Republic of China, Chen Shuibian, discovered in 2006. When commenting on the noteworthy achievements of volunteer groups in Taiwan, Chen used the *chéngyǔ qìngzhú nánshū* 罄竹难书 – 'too numerous to mention'. This soon caused an uproar in linguistic circles on both sides of the Taiwan strait, as many believed that by using this *chéngyǔ*, Chen was comparing volunteer work to criminal behaviour.

The argument concerns the original meaning of the phrase. From the four characters of the *chéngyǔ* alone, there is no negative meaning present. We can see that *qìng* 罄 means 'to exhaust', *zhú* 竹 is 'bamboo', *nán* 难 is 'difficult', and *shū* 书 is 'write'. Literally, the four character phrase means 'unable to write even by using all the bamboo', or in modern terms, 'unable to write it all down on the paper at hand'; or in other words, 'too numerous to record'.

Problems arise when one considers the story behind the phrase. It made its first appearance in the *Annals of Lu*, a historical miscellany of the Spring and Autumn Period. It was used as a way of describing the crimes of an infamous criminal as being too numerous to write down on bamboo slips – which were used as a means of recording the written word before the invention of paper. It is a good example of a *chéngyǔ* that contains important historical background that is not expressed in the four characters alone.

One should always be aware of the proper usage of *chéngyǔ*. The phrase *rìlǐ wànjī* 日理万机, which means 'to attend to thousands of government affairs every day' is another good case in point. It was first used to describe the exacting daily schedule of the Emperor, busy with affairs of governance. People use it today when talking about the work of top national leaders of the Communist party – usage which is considered just about acceptable. If used to describe the work of provincial or local party leaders however, the *chéngyǔ* is not appropriate, as it would be comparing them with the emperors of old, raising them above their station.

The improper use of *chéngyǔ* can also be used for humorous effect. Wei Xiaobao 韦小宝, the protagonist of the best-selling historical fantasy novel *Deer and the Cauldron* by the pre-eminent Chinese novelist Louis Cha, was a character described as being poorly educated. Because of this, he frequently misremembered his *chéngyǔ*, with amusing consequences. One of the most well-known of these mix-ups is his mangling of the saying *yī yán jì chū, sìmǎ nán zhuī* 一言既出，驷马难追, 'a word once spoken cannot be overtaken even by a team of four horses'. This is a very evocative way of saying 'once uttered, words cannot be taken back'. The character *sì* 驷 in this *chéngyǔ* is not commonly used: it is composed of two parts, a horse radical, *mǎ* 马, and the character for four, *sì* 四. Logically, we can see that it means 'a team of four horses'. In the novel, Wei Xiaobao can never quite remember this character, so he instead says '*yī yán jì chū, shénme mǎ nán zhuī* 一言既出，什么马难追'. He replaces the *sì* 驷 with *shénme* 什么, meaning 'anything', giving the new meaning, 'a word once spoken cannot be overtaken by **any** horse'. The beauty of this joke is that the meaning is essentially unchanged, the *chéngyǔ* still makes sense – it has just been 'dumbed down'.

Structure

Four character *chéngyǔ* can be divided into two groups according to their structure: the symmetrical and the asymmetrical. While asymmetrical idioms are not equally balanced, symmetrical idioms tend to follow clear structures.

The following idioms adhere to a noun/verb/noun/verb structure that is quite easy to spot.

- *lóngténg hǔyuè* 龙腾虎跃, literally 'dragons soar and tigers leap', used to refer to 'a scene of bustling activity'.
- *kǒushì xīnfēi* 口是心非, literally 'the mouth says yes, the heart says no', this means 'to say one thing and mean another'.
- *yǎnmíng shǒukuài* 眼明手快, literally 'eyes are bright, hands are quick', this means 'sharp of sight and quick of hand'.

Consider the following *chéngyǔ*, which all conform to a verb/noun/ verb/noun structure:

- *zhǎncǎo chúgēn* 斩草除根, literally 'cut the weeds and dig up the roots', or 'remove the source of the trouble'.
- *páishān dǎohǎi* 排山倒海, literally 'topple the mountains and overturn the seas', or 'earth-shaking'.
- *tōutiān huànrì* 偷天换日, literally 'to steal the sky and change the sun', or 'to perpetrate a huge fraud'.

There are some *chéngyǔ* that are actually just reduplicated words. These are words that are normally two characters that can be 'doubled up' to make *chéngyǔ*. They take an AABB form, so *qīngchǔ* 清楚, 'clear', can become the colloquial *chéngyǔ*, *qīngqīngchǔchǔ* 清清楚楚, 'as plain as day'.

The Chinese *mǎmǎhǔhǔ* 马马虎虎, literally 'horse horse tiger tiger', can be used to describe carelessness or negligence, as well as general mediocrity. It is one of the most frequently used *chéngyǔ* in the Chinese language, and comes from the word *mǎhǔ* 马虎, 'careless'.

As you might expect, there is a good explanation for why something so incongruous as 'horse tiger' has come to mean 'careless' in Chinese. During the Song dynasty, there was a painter who lived in China's capital. The painter would often paint whatever was on his mind at any given moment, sometimes changing his mind mid-painting, and as a result people would frequently struggle to understand his paintings.

One day, he had just finished painting a tiger's head, when he had a visitor who asked him to paint a horse. He then proceeded to paint a horse's body onto the tiger's head. The visitor asked him whether it was a tiger or a horse, to which he replied '*Mǎmǎ hǔhǔ!* 马马虎虎!' Understandably confused, the visitor declined to buy the panting, so the artist hung it in his main hall. The artist's eldest son asked him what it was, to which the man replied 'a tiger', while when his youngest son asked, he said 'a horse'.

The 'horse-tiger' painting

Not long after, his eldest son mistook a horse for a tiger while out hunting, and shot it dead. The artist had no choice but to compensate the owner of the horse for his loss. Worse, his youngest son encountered a tiger in the woods, and believing it to be a horse, tried to mount and ride the beast. The tiger swallowed him whole. The painter was inconsolable, and burned the painting. Ever since, *mǎmǎ hǔhǔ*, or *mǎhǔ* for short, has been a byword for carelessness.

Longer *chéngyǔ*

Some *chéngyǔ* are more than four characters in length. Take for example the five character *wǔshíbù xiào bǎibù* 五十步笑百步, '[the man who retreats] fifty paces laughs at [the man who retreats] one hundred paces'.

The story goes that during the Warring States period, the Chinese philosopher Mencius was discussing philosophy with the King of Liang. In their talk, he made the following analogy: once, there were two soldiers who retreated from the front lines of a battle. One retreated fifty paces, the other ran back one hundred paces. The one who fled fifty paces laughed at the one who had retreated further, calling him a coward. In reality, they had both run away, and so were both in the wrong; it was just a question of degree. It is a metaphor for calling someone out for doing something that one is also guilty of, and is the English equivalent of 'the pot calling the kettle black'.

Other sayings

Proverbs

Proverbs, *yànyǔ* 谚语, are another class of idiom. Unlike *chéngyǔ*, they are mostly complete sentences, and are more colloquial in nature. They are the heritage of thousands of years of primarily agricultural culture, and their meaning is generally quite clear, requiring little explanation. What really separates proverbs from other sayings is their moral function: people use proverbs as a means of telling people what to do or what attitude to take. They reflect the traditional values of a culture. Take the following proverb, for example:

dāo bù mó yào shēngxiù, rén bù xué yào luòhòu 刀不磨要生锈，人不学要落后, 'a knife will rust if not sharpened regularly, a person will fall behind if he does not study'.

This proverb is used to urge someone to keep up with their study, or else they will suffer the fate of a rusty knife – that is, they will become useless.

Two part allegories

A rarer form of Chinese idiom is the *xiēhòuyǔ* 歇后语, the 'two-part allegorical saying'. These are formed from two parts – the first always descriptive, the second carrying the meaning. In this way they are similar to riddles, and guessing the meaning of such a saying is a popular language game in China.

An interesting example of such a saying is the following:

Kǒngfūzǐ bānjiā – jìng shì shū 孔夫子搬家－净是书, 'when Confucius moves house – all he takes are books'

Confucius, the founder of Confucianism and author of some of China's most influential works of classical philosophy and history, was considered the most learned scholar in ancient China. Naturally, he must have had a great many books in his home. No doubt then that when he moved house, what he took with him was mostly piles and piles of books.

This saying is never really used for its literal meaning, however. It's a play on words: here *shū* 书, 'book', has the same pronunciation as *shū* 输, 'to lose', and so when people say *jìng shì shū* 净是书, 'only books', they mean *jìng shì shū* 净是输, 'only lose'. This pun means 'always losing out', and is frequently used at the Mahjong table after a poor run of luck.

One of China's more well-known allegorical sayings alludes to the story of the Eight Immortals Crossing the Sea. The 'Eight Immortals' are a group of legendary beings in Chinese mythology, each possessing magical powers.

DID YOU KNOW?

China has a form of old-fashioned square table, designed for eight people. This kind of table is known as the 'Eight Immortals Table', *bāxiānzhuō* 八仙桌, after the Eight Immortals of legend.

Bāxiān guòhǎi – gèxiǎn shéntōng 八仙过海 – 各显神通, 'Eight Immortals Crossing the Sea – each one displays their special feats'

Eight Immortals Crossing the Sea

According to the legend, the Eight Immortals were one day drinking in a seaside pavilion. Just when the merry-making was at its height, one of the Immortals suggested that they go out together on a voyage across the sea. They all cheered in agreement, and decided to use their special skills to travel across the water, forbidding anyone to be so boring as to take a boat. Han Zhongli took out his magical palm leaf fan, and threw it into the sea. He then jumped on top of it, using the leaf like a raft. He Xiangu threw a lotus into the water, which immediately burst into flower. She stood atop the magical bloom and allowed the waves to whisk her away. In turn, the remaining immortals all used their magical treasures to travel across the seas. The saying is used to mean 'everyone has their own special talents'.

Internet catchphrases

China is home to the world's largest population of internet users, known as 'netizens', or *wǎngmín* 网民 in Chinese. The internet is fertile ground for the coining of catchphrases and buzzwords. These phrases can become popular overnight, and disappear just as quickly. Some stick, and make the transition from the internet to popular culture in general, appearing on television, in films, and everyday conversations across the country.

THE GREAT FIREWALL

China's government censors the internet within its borders using a system known as the Great Firewall of China (*fánghuǒ chángchéng* 防火长城). Access to content that China's authorities deem either harmful to itself or unsuitable for the country's general populace is blocked.

Some of these catchphrases are based on funny sound-bites that have been championed by internet users. The following is one such example: *wǒ shì lái dǎ jiàngyóu de* 我是来打酱油的, 'I'm just here to get soy sauce'.

This phrase is said to have been coined during a Guangzhou television news report, when a man in the street was asked by a journalist for his opinion about internet censorship. In reply, the man said 'It's got nothing to do with me, I'm just out getting soy sauce', either because he really had no opinion on the matter, or because he didn't want to get involved in the debate. The phrase is now used to express wilful ignorance on a certain subject, or when one has nothing to add to the conversation at hand.

Other internet catchphrases originate from China's partiality to homonyms – words that sound the same, but have different meanings. An example is the phrase

'*shénmǎ dōu shì fúyún* 神马都是浮云', which literally means 'mythical horses are all passing clouds'. Literally, this is of course nonsensical – it is a homonym of '*shénme dōu shì fúyún* 什么都是浮云', which means 'everything is passing clouds', or 'everything is short-lived'. It probably emerged from a typo. To type *shénme* 什么, 'what', quickly in Chinese, one can type SM (the initial letters of the pinyin for the two characters) into a pinyin input system. Unfortunately, the shorthand pinyin for the characters *shénmǎ* 神马, 'mythical horses' is also SM, hence the mistake.

An example of usage: *jīnqián, měinǚ zhèxiē dōngxi, shénmǎ dōu shì fúyún* 金钱、美女这些东西，神马都是浮云, 'money, women... these things are all short-lived'.

Looking ahead

Back in the early years of the twentieth century, when reformers called for a new vernacular Chinese literature to replace the old literary Chinese, prominent writer Hu Shi urged his contemporaries to avoid using clichéd sayings, writing 'do not use allusions... do not imitate the ancients'. Hu felt that written Chinese had stagnated, becoming overly-formulaic and lacking in innovation. He implored writers to use their own words in their descriptions, but at the same time he stressed the importance of popular wisdom, saying 'do not avoid popular expressions'. Such popular expressions, whether *chéngyǔ*, proverb, or allegory, have remained a potent part of the Chinese language to the present day. Now, with the increasing popularity of the internet and shorthand forms of communication, there is no doubt that the catchy nature of Chinese sayings will help them remain current for many generations to come, like the 'roc that flies for ten thousand li', *péngchéng wànlǐ*鹏程万里.

Chapter 9:
Etiquette
礼节
lǐjié

Etiquette

礼节

lǐjié

The course of virtue, benevolence, and righteousness cannot be fully carried out without the rules of propriety – **Confucius**

The sage Confucius

Some may find it surprising that rules of etiquette even exist in a country where people bump into one another without as much as an 'excuse me' and queue-cutting has been perfected into a fine art. In fact, China is a very formal country. Traditional etiquette runs much deeper than the surface of modern Chinese life would suggest. Throughout its near 4,000 years of continuous history, China has collected a vast catalogue of rules and regulations governing social behaviour.

These range from the best time to present one's ruler with the gift of a tortoise (not after heavy rainfall), to proper conduct atop a city wall (one should neither point nor shout). In the past, life in China was regulated down to the very last detail. A failure to observe all the rules of etiquette was seen as a breach of the Confucian ethical code, and could result in serious consequences. Fortunately, etiquette in China today is a much more relaxed affair. For example, nobody will give you a strange look if you forget to decline three times before accepting a gift, as tradition requires.

These days, as globalization takes hold over the country, we can see that many of these traditional social rules are no longer observed. In addition, foreigners are not expected to have an understanding of all the ins and outs of Chinese culture. In most situations, it is enough to simply remember to be respectful, while trying one's hardest to *rùxiāng suísú* 入乡随俗 – 'follow the customs of the land'.

CUSTOMS FROM THE ZHOU DYNASTY (C. 1050 – 256 BC)

The following are some historical rules of propriety selected from the Confucian classic, the *Book of Rites* (*Lǐjì* 《礼记》):

Male and female should not use the same towel or comb, nor let their hands touch in giving and receiving.

Rules for arranging dishes for a meal: meat cooked on the bones is set on the left, and the sliced meat on the right; the rice is placed to the left of the guests, and the soup to their right.

When two men are sitting or standing together, do not join them as a third. When two are standing together, another should not pass between them.

He who is sad and anxious should sit with his mat spread apart from others; he who is mourning should sit on a single mat.

Do not saunter about with a haughty gait, nor stand with one foot raised. Do not sit with your knees wide apart, nor sleep on your face.

Introductions

When meeting someone for the first time, it is best to be formal. This is generally good advice for dealing with Chinese people in all situations, as the Chinese tend to look down upon over-enthusiasm and excessive showmanship. In Chinese culture, humility is a virtue.

The traditional Chinese method of greeting someone is to make a bow, with one's hands either clasped in front of the chest or tucked into the sleeves of one's robes. This is known as '*zuòyī* 作揖', but is today outdated, and would be the equivalent of taking one's hat off and bowing from the waist in the West. When first meeting someone, shake hands. The handshake is not, however, as necessary a meeting ritual in China as it is elsewhere. Many people simply nod slightly, or exchange pleasantries instead. As such, a firm handshake does not count as much toward making a good impression as it does in the West. Don't therefore go overboard on a vice-like grip, and likewise don't be put off if the handshake is longer or limper than you would normally expect.

As a general rule, Chinese people wait to be introduced. Self-introductions are seen as uncivilized and unseemly. Within a group, those who aren't mutually acquainted will expect to be introduced to one another by those who are.

Present and receive business cards with both hands, with a slight inclination of the head, showing respect. It's a good idea to have your business card translated into Chinese, or else it may be thrown away very quickly.

Kowtow *KÒUTÓU* 叩头
In ancient Chinese culture, the kowtow – kneeling and bowing so low that one's head touches the ground – was seen as the highest sign of reverence. It was widely used as a means of showing respect for one's elders and superiors. In modern times it is rarely used, and has been practically replaced by bowing.

FÁNWÉN RÙJIÉ 繁文缛节
This idiom is used to refer to over-complicated and trivial rules of etiquette. Over the course of its long and turbulent history, Chinese society has accumulated its fair share of do's and don'ts – which can be deemed *fánwén rùjié*.

Making connections and gaining face

Connections *Guānxì* 关系

Imagine a spider's web, with yourself at the centre, its threads connecting every one of your acquaintances, and with the strongest joints reflecting your strongest relationships. This is a *guānxì* – or 'connections' – network, and to the Chinese mind, every self-respecting person has one. It would be no exaggeration to say that the foundations of modern China are constructed on a billion intertwining webs of *guānxì*.

Personal relationships are central to every aspect of life in China, and for centuries the only way of getting things done was to rely on favours given and returned by family members and acquaintances – contacts in one's *guānxì* network. Those who refuse to play the '*guānxì* game', of making and using one's connections, simply cannot succeed in China – be it at business, in academia, or even in social circles. Recent government attempts to crack down on the practice of using one's *guānxì* to get ahead – in examinations and job interviews, for example – have proven ineffective in tackling what is a serious problem in China.

CHINESE PHRASES RELATED TO GUANXI

lā guānxì 拉关系 – trying to establish a relationship with someone

kào guānxì 靠关系 – to rely on a connection (to get ahead)

qúndài guānxì 裙带关系 – nepotism, or relying on family connections

CHINESE *GUĀNXÌ* KEYWORDS

Guānxì is such a hot topic in China that it has led to its own branch of studies – 'guanxiology' (*guānxìxué* 关系学), and Chinese bookstore shelves are stacked high with self-help books telling one how to go about getting well-connected. 'Guanxiology' can be summed up by the following keywords:

lā 拉: Draw – draw people of use closer to you

tuō 托: Entrust – entrust a task to one of your contacts

pān 攀: Climb – establish *guānxì* with someone of higher social status than oneself

tào 套: Ingratiate – curry favour with people

zuò 做: Do – do people favours

pāi 拍: Fawn – fawn on one's superiors

bài 拜: Respect – pay respect to someone with greater skill, and acknowledge them as a master

gēn 跟: Follow – follow the lead of those who possess *guānxì* one wants to use

péi 培: Cultivate – cultivate your own group of followers

chuàn 串: Connect – connect different contacts together

yìng 应: Nurture – nurture one's *guānxì* with social engagements

xí 袭: Inherit – inherit *guānxì* from one's family, teachers, workplace superiors, etc.

Face *miànzi* 面子

> **SǏ YÀO MIÀNZI HUÓ SHÒUZUÌ** 死要面子活受罪
> 'The desire to keep one's face in death, though endure
> hardship in life', this proverb is used to refer to someone
> who only cares about their face and reputation, at the
> cost of neglecting more basic needs.

Face is similar to the Western idea of reputation: a measure of one's
social status. Having face means that you are respected by your
peers. From a Western perspective, it is very difficult to fully grasp
just how vitally important the role of face is in the day-to-day lives of
the Chinese. To some, it is more important than life itself. In China,
one should always be aware of one's own face, but also make
considerations to preserve the face of others. Losing face is one of
the worst things that can happen to a Chinese person. It is advisable
to never insult, embarrass, shout at, or otherwise demean a person
– especially in public. In order to achieve what you want without
making a Chinese person lose face, criticisms should be delivered
privately and tactfully.

The Chinese concept of face can be divided into the following
categories:

- Having face – *yǒu miànzi* 有面子. The good reputation one earns
  by making wise decisions and avoiding mistakes – something akin
  to personal honour. If one has face, then one's word is as good as
  gold.
- Giving face – *gěi miànzi* 给面子. Certain actions that show
  respect can 'give face' to people – such as paying compliments,
  toasting at a banquet, keeping one's word, and helping someone
  in need.

- Losing face – *diū miànzi* 丢面子. Perhaps something we are all familiar with, this Chinese term has entered the English lexicon. Actions that embarrass or damage can cause one to 'lose face'.
- Saving face – *wǎnhuí miànzi* 挽回面子. Saving face implies a situation where someone's reputation is threatened, or has already been lost, and is subsequently restored. Saving face is an action whereby one proves that they were not in the wrong, or shows that the degree of their wrongdoing was only very small.
- No face – *méi miànzi* 没面子. Similar to losing face, but more serious. Having 'no face' implies that one's reputation is at rock bottom.

> **BÚYÀO LIǍN 不要脸**
> If somebody does something shameless – such as bragging in public, they can be said to be *búyào liǎn* 不要脸, shameless. This literally means 'not wanting face'.

Communication

Subtleties of communication in China

Conversing in China can often feel very disorienting. Chinese people seldom express what they think directly, preferring instead to talk in a more roundabout way, frequently making use of subtext and subtle facial expressions to convey meaning that is quite distinct from what they are actually saying.

Chinese people often feel that a direct 'no' is a source of embarrassment for both parties. They will therefore try to convey disagreement by more indirect methods, such as dodging the question or simply choosing to remain silent. Of course, China has words for 'yes' (*shì* 是) and 'no' (*bù* 不), but they are rarely employed to directly agree or disagree if anything can be left to chance. Fuzzy phrases like 'there may be some slight complications', *kěnéng huì yǒuxiē xiǎowèntí* 可能会有些小问题, or 'I'll consider it', *wǒ kǎolǜ kǎolǜ* 我考虑考虑, are common, when the speaker really means something along the lines of 'that's quite impossible'.

Understanding is not a top priority for the Chinese when dealing with foreigners. If they don't understand something, they will very rarely say so, as 'I don't understand' is seen as a loss of face. It is therefore a good idea to regularly check that you are being understood.

There is a proverb in China that goes '*jiàn rén shuō rénhuà, jiàn guǐ shuō guǐhuà* 见人说人话，见鬼说鬼话'. It means 'upon encountering a person, speak in the person's language, upon encountering a demon, speak in the demon's language'. This proverb shows the need to adjust what one says to one's intended audience, and is a good way of thinking about interpersonal communication in China. It is advisable to avoid certain topics if you want to stay out of trouble with your hosts: sensitive topics such as Tibet, Taiwan, politics, and sex, are best left unmentioned, and criticisms of China in general are not well-received. Outsiders are treated as guests in their country, and it's not the done thing to complain to one's host's face about the way they run their home. Stick to the usual (if rather more stale) conversational favourites, such as Chinese culture and cuisine, places you've been to, and plans for the future, until you are familiar enough with one another to move on to the thornier topics.

SNEEZING

People in ancient China thought that sneezing was a bad omen. Those standing close to the sneezer would try to avoid bad luck by saying something considered lucky, such as '*Hǎo, chángmìng bǎisuì!* 好，长命百岁!', which means 'Good, live to a ripe old age!'

> ### *PĀIMĂPÌ* 拍马屁
> A key weapon in the social armoury of the Chinese is that of flattery – known as *pāimăpì* 拍马屁 – 'slapping the horse's behind'. Top officials and party leaders expect to be flattered wherever they go, and people will use this technique as a way of currying favour with those higher up the social ladder than themselves.

Methods of communication

- Mobile phones: China has more mobile phone users than any other country – being the first nation to reach 900 million users in early 2011. Many families do not have fixed-line telephones, and instead rely on their mobile phones. Don't take offence if someone answers their mobile phone in the middle of a conversation, meeting, or even in the cinema during a particularly tense part of the film. This is perfectly normal in China, and is not considered rude.
- E-mails: Chinese people are increasingly using e-mails to communicate, but for those who do not work in a multinational office environment (read: the majority of the population), daily checking of e-mails has not yet become a habit. Never expect an immediate reply to an e-mail; if you are looking for a quick answer, it would be best to make a phone call.
- QQ instant messaging software: Almost all Chinese people have a 'QQ' instant messaging account on their computers or mobile phones, and most communication that westerners achieve via e-mail is conducted over QQ software in China. In China, one's QQ number is as important as a phone number.

Humour

If you come from a former colonial power, expect upon occasion to be gently ribbed about your country's imperialist past and the injustices inflicted by your forebears upon China. The majority of Chinese bear no grudge against the Western powers (although anti-Japanese sentiment still runs rife), and such jokes should be taken in good spirit. It would be best not to retort with similar jokes mocking aspects of Chinese history, unless you are on very familiar terms.

Chinese people tend to have a good sense of humour, but as most jokes do not translate well into a foreign language, it's advisable to avoid the playful teasing that occurs among friends in the West. Chinese humour tends to focus on situational and physical comedy, with plenty of puns and wordplay. Sarcasm is rarely used, and as such is often misinterpreted.

Formal dinners

The importance of the dinner banquet as a social occasion in China cannot be overstated. It is one of the most frequently occurring forms of social gathering, and to the uninitiated, also one of the most intimidating.

The intensely personal nature of relationships in China, combined with the fact that these relationships must constantly be renewed and strengthened, has resulted in the development of an intricate wining and dining culture, known as '*fànzhuō wénhuà* 饭桌文化'. This custom is so deeply embedded in Chinese culture that people from all walks of life will literally go all out to shower guests with food and drink.

At first, such banquets can be daunting affairs, with their large circular tables and the often unnervingly wide selection of dishes on display, from pigs' brains to ducks' tongues and pretty much every piece of offal in between. Once one gains an understanding of how such occasions work, and the role one is expected to play in them, however, they become much more manageable – even rewarding – experiences. An outsider who gains mastery over the Chinese banquet will, more often than not, find life in China to be much more agreeable than those who do not.

Most business and networking in China is conducted over the dinner table, and a good 'display' at dinner will go a long way towards giving a good impression to your Chinese hosts. At a dinner banquet the Chinese host will traditionally sit facing the door and the guest of honour will be seated directly to his right. Foreign guests will generally be asked to take the first taste of any dish, and don't be surprised if your host piles food into your bowl in an enthusiastic attempt at showing off his nation's culinary culture.

Tips for good etiquette at a Chinese banquet:

- Make it clear at the outset if you don't eat something in particular, are a vegetarian, or don't want to drink.
- Wait until you are invited to eat before tucking in.
- Try to use chopsticks. If you are struggling, use the spoon provided with the bowl or ask for a fork.
- If your chopstick skills momentarily fail you and you drop some food onto the table, smile diffidently and say *bùhǎo yìsī* 不好意思, 'excuse me'.
- Don't put discarded food, such as bones, in the bowl in front of you. Place unwanted food on the plate instead.
- Unless you strongly dislike something, try all of the food that is served, especially when prompted to by your host.
- Identify who the most important member of the party is (usually the person being toasted by the majority of the Chinese guests), and make a toast to them. Touch glasses, and make sure the rim of your glass is lower than that of the recipient of the toast. This shows respect.

Chinese toast with small wine cups

- When toasting your host, or somebody of high social status, empty your glass, saying '*wǒ gānbēi* 我干杯' (I'll drink up), but follow up by saying '*nǐ suíyì* 你随意' (you drink as much as you like) to the target of your toast. This allows them to drink as little, or as much, as they desire, whilst you show your respect and gratitude by emptying your glass. The higher the alcohol content of the drink, and the more of it that you drink, the more 'face' is bestowed upon the host, and indeed to yourself.
- If somebody toasts you, it is rude not to return the toast later on in the course of the meal.
- If you don't like something, it's best not to say so outright. It's best to claim that everything is '*hǎochī* 好吃' (delicious). If you physically can't stomach something and this becomes obvious, say '*wǒ bù xíguàn chī zhège* 我不习惯吃这个' (I'm not used to eating this). Playing this 'cultural difference' card gets you out of eating it whilst saving face for all involved.
- Don't eat the last remaining morsel of food on a dish.
- Leave some rice, or other food, in your bowl when you are finished. If you leave an empty bowl your host will think that you are still hungry and that you have been underfed.
- Be punctual for dinner engagements, as being late is considered very impolite on formal occasions. For casual get-togethers, do not be put off if your Chinese counterparts are late – the Chinese concept of time can be somewhat flexible.

> **ARRIVING ON HORSEBACK**
> When someone says they will arrive '*mǎshàng* 马上', the Chinese word for 'immediately' (literally, this means 'on horseback'), they can mean anything from five minutes to over an hour.

Give, and you shall receive

> *LǏ XIÀ YÚ RÉN, JIĀNG YǑU SUǑ QIÚ* 礼下于人，将有所求
> This proverb means 'when someone proffers a gift, it is because they have a favour to ask'. Gifts, no matter how large or small, are expected to be reciprocated.

The giving and receiving of gifts is an integral part of Chinese relationships. You will be expected to give gifts to those who invite you to dinner, and especially to those with whom you are trying to establish a relationship, be it private or professional.

Presents are traditionally not opened when they are received. The receiver will usually wait until the giver has left before opening the gift. This saves embarrassment for the giver, in case the gift is sub-par, and for the receiver, in case they don't like the gift and are forced to pretend to be grateful. Face saved all round! However, if the giver prompts the receiver to open it up by saying '*dǎkāi kàn yīxià* 打开看一下', 'Go ahead and open it up!', then the receiver will do so.

There are plenty of taboo gifts in China: what you may think is an appropriate present may in fact be an insult wrapped up in a gift box. China's traditionally taboo gifts are mostly associated with

inauspicious homonyms (words that sound the same). Clocks, for
example, are a bad present as the Chinese phrase for 'give a clock',
sòngzhōng 送钟, sounds the same as 'attend a funeral', *sòngzhōng*
送终. Fans (*shàn* 扇) and umbrellas (*sǎn* 伞) are both considered
unlucky because they sound similar to the Chinese *sàn* 散, which
means 'separation', obviously not the best sentiment to express
when giving a gift.

Additionally, one should avoid giving green-coloured headwear as
a gift to a married man – you will be inadvertently calling him a
cuckold! The Chinese saying *dài lǜmào* 戴绿帽, 'wear a green hat',
means that someone's wife has had an affair. It is worth noting
however that in modern China, these already somewhat clichéd
taboos are not always observed.

General gift-giving tips

• The Chinese like 'local speciality produce', so something from your
  native place (biscuits, cigarettes, clothing, preserved food) will
  always go down well. At a pinch, some fresh fruit is always welcome.

• If you are looking to 'slap the horse's behind' and curry favour with
  an important official, you should also consider buying something
  for their spouse. Good gifts for officials' wives are: silk scarves,
  flashy jewellery, and anything from luxury fashion brands.
  Nobody said currying favour was cheap...

• When visiting someone's home (especially in China's rural areas),
  something that can be used around the house will make for a
  thoughtful gift, such as cooking oil.

• Your gift may be refused several times before being accepted,
  out of courtesy. If it is refused more than three times, don't insist.

• When presenting a gift, it is customary to belittle it. Say '*bùchéng jìngyì* 不成敬意', an idiom which means 'it is but a trifle'. Likewise, when receiving a gift, one should praise the magnanimity of the giver, saying '*cǐděng hòulǐ!* 此等厚礼!', which means 'What a generous gift!'

- When giving a gift, never give four of something: the number four (*sì* 四) is considered to be very unlucky, as it sounds very similar to 'death' in Chinese (*sǐ* 死). Eight is a lucky number, so giving eight of something, such as eight pears, is a good thing.

QIĀNLǏ SÒNG ÉMÁO 千里送鹅毛

Literally 'a goose feather sent from afar', this idiom is used to refer to a trifling, yet thoughtful present. During the Tang Dynasty (618–907 AD), local government officials had to pay tribute to the emperor by sending him gifts. One official decided to send several geese to the emperor. The official directed a man named Mian Bogao to escort the geese on their long journey. Mian put the geese in a cage on a fine summer day and started out for the capital, Chang'an (present day Xi'an). The days became hotter and hotter as they travelled. When they came to a lake, Mian Bogao decided to let the geese swim and cool off. But the geese didn't understand his good intentions, and as soon as Mian opened the cage, they flew into the sky, leaving only a few feathers on the ground. Distraught, all he could do was pick up a goose feather and head for Chang'an. The gift of a meagre feather puzzled everyone at the court. But after Mian explained the situation, instead of punishment, the emperor gave him a handsome reward. When you think a gift to someone is lacking in monetary value, you can say '*qiānlǐ sòng émáo* 千里送鹅毛' to nevertheless express your sincerity.

qiānlǐ sòng émáo

Clothing etiquette

A stroll down any street in today's China can be a bewildering experience for the more fashion conscious visitor. Men with one trouser leg rolled up, women with sleeve protectors over their jackets, and nappyless toddlers ambling around in open-crotch trousers are all perfectly common sights. Aware of the fashion *faux-pas* routinely being committed by its citizens, the municipal government of Shanghai tried to crack down on the practice of wearing pyjamas outdoors before the Shanghai Expo in 2010 – to little lasting effect. For many Chinese, comfort trumps style.

Colours and dress

Colour plays an important part in Chinese culture, and there are many superstitions and traditions surrounding the various colours. It's a good idea to pay attention to these when choosing one's wardrobe for a formal function. For non-formal occasions however, pretty much anything goes.

- White (*bái* 白) – it is best to avoid wearing all-white suits or dresses, as white represents death and is thus the traditional colour for funerary garments in China. A white shirt or blouse is best paired with trousers or skirt of a different colour.
- Red (*hóng* 红) – red is traditionally a very lucky colour, and is strictly forbidden at funerals as it is symbolic of happiness. A splash of red on an outfit, say on a tie or scarf, will go down well, however avoid an entirely red outfit as this will give the impression that you are attending a wedding – as the bride or groom! Many Chinese have lucky red socks or underwear.
- Black (*hēi* 黑) – the Taiji symbol uses black and white to represent the unity of Yin and Yang, and ancient Chinese people regarded black as the most important of all the colours. Ancient Taoist philosopher Lao Zi said that 'the five colours blind the eye', so the Taoists chose black as the representative colour of the Tao, their religion. In modern China, black is used in daily clothing.
- Yellow (*huáng* 黄) – in China, yellow is considered to be the most beautiful colour. Yellow was the official colour of Imperial China, and is viewed as symbolic of the five legendary emperors – the chief among whom was *Huángdì* 黄帝, the Yellow Emperor. Yellow is used as decoration in royal palaces, on altars and temples, and yellow was the primary colour of the emperor's attire, the Dragon Robe. Yellow also represents freedom from worldly desires, and is a key colour in Buddhism. Monks' robes are ochre – an orangey-yellow colour, and parts of Buddhist temples are painted yellow.

YĪGUĀNBÙZHĚNG 衣冠不整
This idiom literally means 'one's cap and robe not in proper order'; which is a way of saying 'sloppily dressed'.

TRADITIONAL CHINESE DRESS

Qípáo 旗袍 – the original *qípáo* was a traditional one-piece dress worn by Manchu women during the Qing Dynasty. It was loose-fitting and hung straight down the body. The more stylish, tightly fitting *qípáo*, or cheongsam, that is popular today was the creation of fashionable socialites in 1920's Shanghai.

Zhongshan Suit, *Zhōngshānzhuāng* 中山装 – a style of tunic suit made famous by Chairman Mao, but first introduced as a form of national dress by Sun Yat-sen after the founding of the Republic of China. It is known in the West as the Mao suit, but in China as the Zhongshan suit. After the establishment of the People's Republic in 1949, the suit was widely worn by government leaders as a symbol of proletarian unity, and for a time became a counterpart to the Western business suit. Although they fell out of fashion in the 1990s, they retain a retro chic and are still occasionally worn by Chinese leaders at important functions.

Chapter 10:
Festivals
节日
jiérì

Festivals

节日
jiérì

> *The end of the year according to the lunar calendar is, after all, the right time for a year to end. A strange almost-new-year sort of atmosphere seems to overlay everything; pale grey clouds at evening, against which flash the hot little fires of crackers giving a thunderous boost to the kitchen god's ascent into heaven. And as one draws into it the scene grows noisier, and scattered on the air is the sting of gunpowder.*
>
> **Benediction** by Lu Xun (translated by Edgar Snow)

The Chinese have a word to describe a lively, bustling atmosphere – *rènào* 热闹. The two characters that come together to make this word mean 'heat' (*rè* 热) and 'noise' (*nào* 闹), and these are generally fitting words to describe a Chinese festive scene or gathering. In modern times, 'hot and noisy' fireworks are used to celebrate almost every festival in China, although many other ancient traditions are also observed. The Chinese like to *kàn rènào* 看热闹, literally 'see the hubbub' – that is, to go where the crowds are and participate in the festivities. The streets are normally most *rènào* during festivals and holidays, which are still observed with religious devotion in China. China's traditional festivals are closely tied to its traditional calendar, and serve to mark the changing seasons throughout the year.

The Chinese character for 'year', *nián* 年, in its earliest form, was a depiction of a person bringing in the grain – the grain harvest, which is done once a year. Another term for the traditional Chinese lunisolar calendar is the 'agricultural calendar': *nónglì* 农历. The agricultural year is divided into 12 lunar months, based on the phases of the moon, and each month consists of either 29 or 30 days. The first month of the year is known as *zhēngyuè* 正月, and the last is customarily known as *làyuè* 腊月. The dates of China's traditional holidays are calculated using the agricultural calendar, while the Gregorian calendar is used for all official business and modern festivities.

Each year of the Chinese calendar is 'governed' by one of the 12 animals of the Chinese zodiac, which are rotated in a 12-year cycle. Your birth animal is an important part of your identity in China, and people will often ask one another *nǐ shǔ shénme?* 你属什么? – 'what animal sign are you?'. It is believed that one's animal sign dictates one's personality, and can bring good or bad fortune depending on the year. 'Rats' are generally seen as being witty, charming people, while 'tigers' are brave and highly competitive, for example. Most parents prefer sons born in the year of the dragon. The year of one's birth animal is known as *běnmìngnián* 本命年, and is on the whole thought to bring misfortune. Aside from the years, each month, day, and two-hour period also has its respective animal sign, a system which can lead to very complicated astrological readings.

Spring Festival *Chūnjié* 春节

Spring Festival marks the beginning of the traditional Chinese year. The date of the new year is determined by the Chinese lunisolar calendar. A time for reunion, reconciliation, and goodwill, it is the longest and most important celebration in the Chinese calendar.

The origins of Spring Festival can be traced back to Chinese legend. According to the story, a long time ago, a vicious beast lived in the mountains. Not only did it prey upon wild animals, but the beast also had a taste for people – especially young children. The beast was known as '*Nián*' 年, the Chinese word for 'year'.

The 12 animal signs of the Chinese zodiac (from left to right, top to bottom): rat, ox, tiger, rabbit, dragon, snake, horse, ram, monkey, chicken, dog, and pig

Every year on Chinese New Year's Eve, Nian would run amok in the village, preying on livestock and villagers alike. The people came to call this particular time of year the *niánguān* 年关, the 'yearly ordeal'. In time, every New Year's Eve, each family would gather together and prepare a large feast. They would secure the chicken coops and cow sheds, and bolt their front doors. Hiding inside their homes, they ate the New Year's Eve family dinner. When the beast Nian arrived, the streets were empty, and all the homes were boarded up. By the time the cockerel crowed with the dawn, all it could do was run back to the mountains. Having survived their yearly ordeal, the people would rush out of their homes in celebration, congratulating their neighbours and letting off firecrackers.

Eventually, people learned that Nian was afraid of the colour red, bright lights, and loud noises. So it was that every New Year, households would put up couplets written on red paper, raise red lanterns, wear red clothes, and let off firecrackers – all now traditional Spring Festival activities. If they did so, the beast would not dare come down from the mountain.

Spring Festival taboos

It is considered unlucky to say a number of Chinese words on the first day of Spring Festival. Some of these are: *pò* 破, 'broken', *sǐ* 死, 'death', *guǐ* 鬼, 'ghost', *shā* 杀, 'kill', and *bìng* 病, 'illness'. It is also taboo for babies and young children to cry, because crying can represent imminent disaster. If a child cries on the first day of New Year, the child cannot be beaten or reprimanded for fear of them continuing to cry even more.

- One must take particular care not to break any crockery during the New Year period. Water must not be spilled, and the jar used to store rice must not be left empty.
- Medicine must not be taken on the first day of the new year, as this implies that one will be taking it all year along.

A Spring Festival calendar: what to do and when to do it

The week before New Year
In the days before the festivities begin, people will give their homes a thorough 'spring clean', animals will be slaughtered and food supplies stockpiled, all in preparation for the coming holiday.

New Year's Eve
Spring Festival couplets will be stuck up on door-frames. The practice of displaying Spring Festival couplets dates back to the Qin dynasty, when peach wood charms were hung up on either side of the front door. Rhyming couplets were not written until around the Five

Dynasties period in the tenth century AD. The couplets are hand-picked – and often hand-written – and displayed either side of the front door of each household, whether it be in the inner city or remote countryside. They are read from top to bottom, and the first line is pasted on the right-hand side of the door, the second line on the left-hand side of the door.

Couplets should have a matching rhythm and both lines should be of the same length. An example of a simple couplet would be:

> *Xìngfú jíxiáng,*
> 幸福吉祥，
> Happiness and good fortune,
> *Huākāi fùguì*
> 花开富贵
> Riches and honour in full bloom

One of the main events of Spring Festival is the New Year's Eve dinner. Young and old will gather around the table to eat the most lavish dinner of the year. Although the dishes eaten at this dinner differ from region to region, most dinners will have two necessary constituents: hot pot and fish. Chinese hot pot is a pot of boiling soup, into which raw vegetables and meats are added and cooked at the table. The tradition of eating fish comes from another homophone in Chinese: *yú* 鱼, 'fish', sounds like *yú* 余, 'plenty'. Thus eating fish at New Year symbolizes *niánnián yǒuyú* 年年有余, 'having plenty every year'. After dinner, families will stay up to welcome in the new year – adults will chat and watch television, and children will play or go to bed early, only to be woken later in the night as the celebrations intensify.

New Year's Day

The Chinese have a custom of letting off firecrackers on the first day of New Year. Known as *kāimén bàozhú* 开门爆竹, literally 'opening the door and setting off firecrackers', this has been practised for over 2,000 years. Modern-day fireworks are simply an evolution of this ancient tradition. Firecrackers are set off upon opening one's door on the morning of New Year's Day – sometimes in the very early hours. This tradition is also observed when shops open for business later in the holiday. Considering the fireworks most households let off through the night, and intermittently throughout most of the two-week holiday, Spring Festival is not a great time to catch up on one's beauty sleep.

NEW YEAR'S GREETINGS

Here's how to offer your best wishes for the new year:

Gōngxǐ fācái 恭喜发财 – 'Wishing you a prosperous New Year'

Xīnnián kuàilè 新年快乐 – 'Happy New Year'

Xīnnián hǎo 新年好 – 'Have a good New Year'

In ancient China, people would kowtow to the elders of their family upon waking up on the first day of the new year. The elders, after receiving the respects of their descendants, would then prepare *yāsuìqián* 压岁钱 – money given to children as a New Year gift. Although the kowtowing has died out, the practice of giving money has not. The money is given in red envelopes. Younger generations will prepare gifts for their elders, and the Spring Festival gift industry is a huge one in China. Although it is comparable to the Christmas tradition of gift-giving, Spring Festival gifts are normally bought for one's parents or grandparents, and as such, vitamins and other health products are popular presents.

People will then go to the houses of their close relatives and friends to extend New Year's greetings. It is traditional to bring presents to one's nearest and dearest. Priority visits are made to the elder generations of the family – the parents, grandparents, and great-grandparents. Those with extended families will normally split up their family visits over the whole New Year period, with closest relatives being visited first.

It is also a tradition to celebrate the new year with new clothes, symbolic of a fresh beginning, which are worn on this day.

> ***ZHĀNGDĒNGJIÉCĂI*** 张灯结彩
> This idiom, which means 'decorated with lanterns and coloured banners', can be used to describe a typical Spring Festival scene.

Second day
On the second day, sacrifices are made to the God of Wealth to ensure prosperity in the coming year. These sacrifices involve burning paper money, and making offerings of pork, chicken, lamb, duck, and red carp. Wonton soup should be eaten at lunchtime.

Third day
The third day of the new year is the day of the ram – legend has it that this is the day Nü Wa, the female deity that created mankind from a lump of clay, made sheep. People should not slaughter sheep on this day, and good weather indicates that sheep-rearing households will have a prosperous year.

Fifth day
People in the north of China eat dumplings (*shuǐjiǎo* 水饺) on the fifth day. This is also the reputed birthday of the God of Wealth, and the day many businesses choose to reopen.

Seventh day
The seventh day commemorates the birthday of mankind, and on this day people traditionally eat 'seven treasure soup', a thick rice soup made with seven seasonal vegetables. Fine weather on this day

indicates happiness for the general populace in the year to come.

Eighth day
The eighth day is the birthday of grain crops in Chinese legend. Fine weather on this day foretells a good harvest in the coming year. Parents will take children out into the fields to see the over-wintering crops and to learn about farm work. Rice or noodles are traditionally eaten for dinner.

Ninth day
This is the birthday of the Yellow Emperor, and sacrifices will be made to him.

Tenth day
The tenth day is the birthday of stone, and as such, grindstones, pestles and mortars are not to be touched, else it is said calamity may come to the crops.

Fifteenth day
The fifteenth day is Lantern Festival, and marks the end of the Chinese New Year festivities.

Modern elements

Ever since 1982, China's state television has held a New Year's gala, broadcast at eight pm on New Year's Eve. The New Year's gala is the most-watched television event of the whole year, and is a mixture of comedy skits, song and dance routines, acrobatics performances, and other traditional arts. Because of its broad target audience (read: all Chinese people under the sun), content can be hit and miss. It has its critics, but it has become something of an institution. Even those families who don't have any interest in watching will probably have it on in the background whilst the adults chat and the children play.

Spring Festival is the most important time of year for families.

It is a time of reunion in a country where many are forced by economic necessity to work away from home. When China's huge population of migrant workers heads home for the holidays, the country's fairly impressive, and mostly reliable, transport system tends to grind to an overburdened halt. Train tickets become almost impossible to buy, and if, by some stroke of luck, you do manage to acquire a ticket, it will likely be standing-room only in a carriage packed with crying babies, screeching children, and a hazy fog of cigarette smoke. Everyone will be carrying over-sized packages of over-priced gifts for their families, leaving little room for people to sit or even stand. This is *chūnyùn* 春运, the 'Spring Festival travel season', and it is quite an experience.

A traditional Spring Festival scene

FÚ 福

Chinese people have a custom of hanging an upside-down character *fú* 福 on their door during the Festival period. This implies that they will have good fortune in the year to come. One year, the Ming dynasty emperor Zhu Yuanzhang planned to use the character *fú* to mark a person as a target for assassination. The empress caught wind of his plan, and to avert this disaster, she secretly ordered all the citizens in the city to hang the letter on their doors. One household happened to be illiterate, and pasted the character on upside down. The Emperor was furious upon hearing this news, and ordered the execution of everyone who lived in that particular household. The Empress, thinking quickly, explained that they hung the character upside down on purpose, as it signifies the arrival of good fortune – *fúdào* 福到. In Chinese, *fú* is fortune, and *dào* is 'arrive'. The word for 'upside down' is *dào* (倒), which sounds similar to *dào*, 'arrive'. The Emperor was appeased, and nobody was executed. The 'upside-down *fú*' quickly caught on across the country.

Lantern Festival *Yuánxiāojié* 元宵节

The tradition of the Lantern Festival marking the end of the New Year's festivities dates back some 2,000 years, to the Western Han dynasty when the Emperor Ming of Han was on the throne. The emperor, who was a Buddhist, had heard that monks would light lanterns to venerate Buddha on the 15th day of the first month – the first full moon of the year. He ordered that lanterns be hung up around the palace, and in all the temples of the land as a way of promoting the spread of Buddhism. Later, the gentry and common citizens alike began hanging their own lanterns on that night. A religious festival thus became a secular celebration, a night to enjoy the full moon and the gorgeous displays of multi-coloured lanterns.

The festival has grown in length and importance over the years, from taking place on only a single night in Han times, to being spread over three days during the Tang dynasty, and further extended to five days in the Song dynasty. In Ming dynasty times, lanterns were lit on the eighth day of the month, and only brought down on the 17th day. By the Qing dynasty, dragon and lion dances, stilt walking, and other performances had been added to the traditional celebrations – but the festivities had been cut back to four or five days in length.

The lanterns themselves are the main attraction of this festival. People will walk about the town or village, taking in the sights of the various lanterns that are hung from the tiled eaves. Predominantly red in colour, they are made from all kinds of materials, such as paper, silk, porcelain, or even white jade, and some depict folk stories and scenes from legend. As with Christmas lights in the West, some parts of China take the lantern festival more seriously than others, and Junqi village in Hebei province is one such place. Each year, all the households in the village will make lanterns to hang in the courtyards of their homes or by their front doors. Some will hang lanterns from tall poles, known as 'sky lanterns', that attract villagers from far and wide.

During the Lantern Festival it is customary to eat sticky rice dumplings, known as *yuánxiāo* 元宵 or *tāngyuán* 汤圆. They are little round balls made from glutinous rice flour, and can have a variety of fillings, either sweet or savoury. They signify reunion and togetherness.

Lantern Riddles

Guessing lantern riddles is a popular game that is played at this time of year. The riddles are usually written on the lanterns, and passers-by will try and guess the answer. The tradition began during the Southern Song dynasty, in Hangzhou, a city which was known as the 'lantern capital'. The following are examples of simple riddles:

duō yībàn 多一半, 'half as much again'
Answer: *xī* 夕, 'evening'

This riddle requires a good knowledge of Chinese in order to solve it. It consists of the character *duō* 多, 'much or many', followed by *yībàn* 一半, 'half'. If you take away half of the character *duō*, you are left with *xī* 夕, 'evening', and you have your answer. More straightforward riddles are also common:

Méiyǒu jiǎo, méiyǒu shǒu, bēiqǐ fángzi jiù huì zǒu. 没有脚、没有手，背起房子就会走。 'No feet and no hands, but carrying its house it can go on its way.'
Answer: *wōniú* 蜗牛, 'snail'

DID YOU KNOW?

The dragon dance (*wǔlóng* 舞龙) is a traditional part of the Lantern Festival. In South China, the dragon dance will be performed along the streets of the villages. The 'dragon' is carried by a team of performers, each holding a part of the dragon on a pole. Usually, the dragon will stop at people's doors, and nod its head up and down before performing a few rhythmic movements, wishing the inhabitants of the house a happy New Year. It is customary for the master of the house to let off firecrackers or fireworks in response, and give the performers either a tip in a red envelope, or a suitable gift – or else suffer the consequences of angering the 'dragon'.

Qingming Festival *Qīngmíngjié* 清明节

Qingming Festival marks the start of spring in the Chinese calendar. The Chinese name, *Qīngmíng* 清明, can be translated as Clear Bright Festival, which brings to mind the clear, crisp springtime air, the enjoyment of which is all part of the festivities. While spring is a season of growth and renewal, the festival also calls for reflection and remembrance, for it is also known as **Tomb Sweeping Day**. At Qingming, families will go to the tombs of their ancestors to pay their respects and sweep away the dirt and debris that has collected over the past year. Chinese family tombs are normally located on hillsides surrounding centres of population, in places that are deemed to have good fengshui. Since 2009, Qingming has been the focus of a three-day national holiday.

The practice of 'tomb sweeping' – *sǎomù* 扫墓 in Chinese – involves clearing away weeds, replacing the earth around the tomb, offering up sacrifices, such as burning paper money, and performing simple ceremonies to pay one's respects. Qingming falls on the 104th day after the winter solstice – usually around 5 April in the Gregorian calendar.

Aside from sweeping tombs, Qingming is the time to celebrate the arrival of warm weather, to say goodbye to the long, cold winter, and revel in the budding greenery of spring. In the past, this celebration was known as *tàqīng* 踏青 literally 'stepping on the green', and people would use this festival as an excuse to get out into the countryside and enjoy walks in the woods and hills. These days, this practice has evolved into the 'spring outing', *chūnyóu* 春游, in which schools, companies, and families will organize trips to popular tourist destinations both at home and abroad.

> **DID YOU KNOW?**
>
> *Along the River During the Qingming Festival*
> (*Qīngmíng shànghétú* 清明上河图) is one of China's
> most famous paintings. It is a long scroll painting that
> was completed in the Northern Song dynasty, and depicts
> a traditional Qingming scene. Over 1,500 individual
> figures can be seen in the painting, which is split into four
> parts – 'walking in the hills', 'going boating on the river',
> 'going to the market', and 'sweeping the tombs'. Each part
> depicts a different aspect of the festival, and it has helped
> modern historians to understand how the festival was
> celebrated in ancient China. Overpriced copies of this
> painting can be found at souvenir stalls in most of
> China's major tourist attractions.

Dragon Boat Festival *Duānwǔjié* 端午节

The Dragon Boat Festival, known also as Duanwu Festival, is held on
the fifth day of the fifth lunar month. This is the summer solstice,
when the days are at their longest in the northern hemisphere and
the sun is considered to be at its strongest.

Many believe that the festival is held to honour the memory of the
Chinese poet Qu Yuan 屈原 (340–278). Qu Yuan is a tragic figure in
Chinese history. He was a top statesman of the kingdom of Chu
during the Warring States period (475–221 BC), and sworn enemy of
the oppressive state of Qin. When the king of Chu decided to ally with
the powerful Qin, Qu Yuan was banished for his opposition to the
alliance. Spending decades in exile, Qu Yuan composed some of
China's most heartfelt and evocative poetry – collectively known as
the *Odes of Chu* (*Chǔcí* 《楚辞》). Qin went on to betray the king of
Chu, and captured the Chu capital. Hearing of the downfall of his
homeland, Qu Yuan's grief was so intense that he committed suicide,

throwing himself into a river on the fifth day of the fifth month. Ever since, the day has become a time to celebrate his life and works. People race dragon boats, and throw bamboo leaf-wrapped rice cakes, known as *zòngzi* 粽子, into the rivers. It is said that this prevents the fish from eating Qu Yuan's body.

Chinese people have in fact celebrated the Dragon Boat Festival since before Qu Yuan's time, and its real origins can likely be linked to totemic dragon worship. In Chinese mythology, the dragon is the symbol of male 'yang' energy, or sunshine, and they are said to habitually live in China's lakes and rivers. The rice cakes represent an offering to the dragon king, and the dragon boat races naturally serve as a form of reverence.

While dragon boat races are not as widespread or ceremonious as they once were, the traditional rice cakes, *zòngzi*, are still central to the celebrations. *Zòngzi* are made from glutinous rice, but their methods of preparation and fillings may vary from place to place. Sichuan *zòngzi* are known for their hot and spicy taste, while *zòngzi* from the Southern province of Hainan are wrapped in banana leaves instead of the traditional bamboo leaves.

Mid-Autumn Festival *Zhōngqiūjié* 中秋节

If the Dragon Boat Festival is a time for celebrating the sun and the onset of summer, then Mid-Autumn Festival is all about the moon. The waxing and waning of the moon dictates the passing of the months in China's agricultural calendar, and the moon holds a special place in the hearts of the Chinese. Mid-Autumn Festival falls on the 15th of the eighth lunar month, when the moon is at its fullest.

The moon's full, round shape on this day symbolizes family reunion, and the Mid-Autumn Festival is a time for families to gather together. Sons and daughters will return home – if the time-frame of the official holiday permits – and those who live abroad may make the long journey back to China in time to celebrate with their loved ones. Chinese people believe the moon will be even brighter when viewed from their home town.

The festival traces its roots back to the Zhou dynasty, when the emperor would offer sacrifices to the sun during springtime and to the moon during the autumn. Mid-Autumn is also the most poetic of China's holidays. The moon has long been a central motif in Chinese poetry, from Li Bai's Tang dynasty refrains to the *cí* 词 poems of Su Dongpo in the Song dynasty. Indeed, popular legend has it that Li Bai was so fond of the moon that it brought about his death. It is said he drowned while trying to embrace the reflection of the moon in the Yangtze River – perhaps after a little bit too much to drink.

Night Thoughts by *Li Bai*
I wake, and moonbeams play around my bed, Glittering like hoar-frost to my wandering eyes; Up towards the glorious moon I raise my head, Then lay me down – and thoughts of home arise. (Translated by Herbert A. Giles)

Moon cakes

Moon cakes are round pastries with an egg yolk filling, primarily eaten on and around Mid-Autumn Festival. They are said to represent the moon, and biting into a moon cake is like taking a bite out of the moon itself. Moon cakes have become big business in recent years. It is customary to send moon cakes to one's friends and family, as well as business associates and superiors. The giving of moon cakes is now part of China's culture of 'face', and the more money that is spent on a beautifully-designed box of handmade moon cakes, the more 'face' one can gain by gifting it to someone. Like all popular traditions, moon cakes have evolved with the changing times. These days, moon cakes come in a variety of flavours, from those with traditional lotus paste fillings to ice cream and coffee varieties.

MOON CAKES VS. THE MONGOLS

The innocuous moon cake may have played a role in shaping China's history – China has a number of folk tales concerning the use of moon cakes as a means of smuggling secret, revolutionary messages. When China was ruled by the Mongols of the Yuan dynasty (1280–1368 AD), large group gatherings were banned. Noting that the Mongols did not eat moon cakes, the Ming revolutionaries formulated a plan to hold an uprising on the 15th day of the eighth month, Mid-Autumn Festival. The revolutionaries distributed moon cakes to all the Chinese residents of the capital. The moon cakes were used to hide a secret message coordinating the Chinese revolt. The Mongols, caught off guard, were defeated, and the Ming dynasty (1368–1644) was established.

Double Ninth Festival *Chóngyángjié* 重阳节

The Double Ninth Festival, also known as Chongyang Festival, occurs on the ninth day of the ninth lunar month. In Chinese numerology, nine is associated with the yang, or male energy, while the number six is associated with the yin, or female energy. The ninth day of the ninth month is therefore named *chóngyáng* 重阳, or 'repeated yang'.

One of the main traditions of the festival is to climb up to a high place and take in the view, known as *dēnggāo* 登高 ('climbing high'). This comes from the Eastern Han dynasty superstition that climbing up to a high place, while carrying a sprig of Japanese dogwood (the *zhūyú* 茱萸 plant) and drinking chrysanthemum wine once atop the hill, would help avoid bad luck. Both chrysanthemums and *zhūyú* are believed to possess cleansing qualities and can also be used to air out houses and cure illnesses.

The tradition of climbing to a high point – which has been upheld by emperors of China throughout history – has today evolved into the practice of climbing nearby mountains. It is a means of getting some exercise before the onset of winter, and taking in the autumn scenery.

During the festival, people traditionally eat Chongyang cake (*chóngyánggāo* 重阳糕), rice flour cakes. The word for 'cake', *gāo* 糕, is also a homonym for *gāo* 高, high, as in 'climbing high'. Chrysanthemum wine is a drink associated with this festival, as chrysanthemums are in bloom in the ninth lunar month. Chrysanthemums are a symbol of longevity, and people believe that drinking the wine on the ninth day of the ninth month will help them to lead a long life.

There is a folk saying in the northern province of Shandong that is related to this aspect of the festival: *jiǔyuè jiǔ, jiǔ chóngyáng, júhuā zuòjiǔ mǎn gāng xiāng* 九月九，九重阳，菊花做酒满缸香, which means 'On the ninth day of the ninth month, on the double ninth, the wine jars brim with the aroma of chrysanthemums.'

> ### DID YOU KNOW?
> Aside from the main national festivities, many of China's ethnic minorities have their own festivals that are celebrated throughout the year. Some of the strangest – and most interesting – minority festivals include Naadam, a Mongolian festival held in the summer months, and celebrated with large-scale wrestling, horse racing, and archery competitions, or the water-splashing festival, which marks the new year for the Dai ethnic group who live in Southern Yunnan province.

APPRECIATING CHRYSANTHEMUMS

According to Chinese tradition, for it to be considered a superior specimen, a chrysanthemum plant should be planted in its own pot, be one foot high, and one foot in diameter. From the side, its branches should not be visible, and from the top, the soil should be covered by foliage.

Modern-day festivities

Aside from the traditional festivities that occur throughout the year, China has a number of modern celebrations that are observed throughout the year. China celebrates international worker's day, known as Labour Day, *láodòngjié* 劳动节, on 1 May. This is a holiday for all those who have arguably made the biggest contribution to China's rapid development – the migrant workers – to take some time off. Modern China celebrates its birthday every year on 1 October with a three-day national holiday, known as National Day (*guóqìngjié* 国庆节). This commemorates the founding of the People's Republic of China on 1 October 1949, with a ceremony at Tian'anmen Square. Smaller festivities such as Women's Day (*fùnǚjié* 妇女节) and Children's Day are also observed, either with half days at work for women or a day off from school for children.

China's rising affluence, together with the influence of globalization and the Chinese love of *rènào* 热闹, has led to the ever-increasing importance of Western festivals. Christmas and New Year, as well as International Valentine's Day, have all become firmly entrenched in the Chinese calendar, although the original meaning of these festivals has mostly become lost in a wave of commercialization.

While it may seem that the end result of this overload of festivities would be something akin to 'festival burn-out', or at least a mild case of the humbugs, Chinese people generally treat their major festivals with a solemn dedication to tradition, all the while holding an insatiable curiosity toward the relatively unfamiliar festivals of the Western world.

Chapter 11:
Culinary culture
饮食文化
yǐnshí wénhuà

Culinary culture

饮食文化
yǐnshí wénhuà

An impatient man cannot eat hot beancurd.
Chinese proverb

Confucius said, 'Food is the first necessity of man'. Eating, and the culture surrounding it, is an indispensable part of Chinese life. In China, the dinner table is host to all manner of human experience: around it, business deals are won and lost, romances played out and feuding families reconciled.

This preoccupation with food is reflected in China's spoken language. One of the most commonly heard greetings in China is 'have you eaten yet?' (*nǐ chīle méi?* 你吃了没？) – this indicates the overriding concern with the state of fullness of one's belly in Chinese culture. Additionally, China's language conceptualizes a range of emotions and ideas in the vocabulary of 'eating'. The ability to bear hardship is known as *chīkǔ* 吃苦, or literally, 'eating bitterness'. If someone is startled, they are described as *chījīng* 吃惊, literally 'eat a shock', and if one loses out, they are said to *chīkuī* 吃亏, or 'eating a loss'. More colloquially, 'eating tofu', *chī dòufu* 吃豆腐, can mean 'to flirt with a woman'.

The first archaeological traces of people using fire to cook food can be found in China. Peking Man, who lived some half a million years ago, may have roasted his meat. From humble beginnings, the country's culinary culture wasted no time in developing to epic proportions. By the Zhou dynasty, the imperial palace employed over 2,000 people tasked with the job of feeding the royal court. China's culinary culture has since directly influenced the cuisine of countries across Asia, such as Japan, Korea, Mongolia, Thailand, and Singapore; and indirectly influenced the way people eat in almost every country in the world.

China has suffered many periods of drought and famine in the course of its history, and during such times of need, the people would eat anything that they could lay their hands on. A well-trodden Chinese idiom is *jī bù zé shí* 饥不择食, which means 'when hungry you don't pick and choose what you eat'. Many aspects of Chinese cuisine as it exists today were thus first born out of necessity, and have sometimes led to interesting discoveries, like the remarkable medicinal properties of the ginseng root. In fact, botanists have claimed that Chinese people eat over six hundred different kinds of vegetables – six times the number of varieties eaten in the West. For common folk in ancient China, meat dishes were only eaten on very special occasions, such as the major festivals of the year. People were forced by their economic circumstances to eat a diet that mostly consisted of vegetables. There are more edible vegetables, and, perhaps more importantly, ways of cooking them in China than can probably be recorded.

A basic principle of Chinese cuisine is to 'make the most of every ingredient'. Whether the raw ingredient is an animal or a plant, a Chinese chef will be able to use practically every part of it. The heads and feet of animals, as well as their viscera and even blood, are never wasted. Likewise, the roots, stem, leaves, and even flowers of plants and vegetables are all used in Chinese cooking. Prawn shells left over after the flesh has been peeled can be used in the dish known as 'three prawn tofu' *sānxiā dòufu* 三虾豆腐, and fish scales can be blended to make 'crystal meat purée', *shuǐjīng kuài* 水晶脍.

> ### NAMING ONE'S FOOD
>
> The naming of dishes can be almost as important as the taste of the food itself. Each specific dish has its own, often poetic, name. Take the simple cold dish of sliced tomato, to which a sprinkling of white sugar is added. This is known in some areas as *huǒshān báiyún* 火山白云, or 'white clouds above the red volcanoes'. Chicken's feet, a popular Chinese snack, are called *fèngzhuǎ* 凤爪, literally 'phoenix talons'. China even has dishes named after poets themselves, such as Dongpo pork (*Dōngpōròu* 东坡肉), named after the famed Song dynasty poet, Su Dongpo 苏东坡, who invented the dish during his exile in the southern city of Hangzhou.

Chopsticks

One thing most people know about Chinese food is that it is eaten with chopsticks – small, tapered sticks of equal length. Children learn to use chopsticks from an early age, starting with 'trainer chopsticks' that are shorter than average. Longer chopsticks can be used in cooking, to stir dishes in a wok for example.

Chopsticks are normally more suited to Chinese food than Western food, as anyone who has tried to eat a whole steak with chopsticks can attest. However, when it comes to eating fish whole, as they are eaten in China, nothing beats a nimble pair of chopsticks for prying small bits of flesh away from the bones. Chopsticks are equally adept at plucking the fish's eye from its socket, should you have a taste for it. Chopsticks should never be stuck into a bowl of rice so that they stand up, as this resembles incense sticks stuck in ash – a way of mourning the dead. Resting the chopsticks over the top of one's bowl signifies that one has had enough.

The first historical record of chopsticks can be found in the *Records of the Grand Historian* (*Shǐjì* 《史记》), which states that King Zhou of the Shang Dynasty, who lived over 3,000 years ago, used a pair of chopsticks carved from ivory. The old word for chopsticks was *zhù* 箸, but it was believed this sounded too similar to the word for 'cease', *zhù* 住, so they came to be known as *kuàizi* 筷子. If you are struggling with chopsticks, small spoons are readily available in most restaurants. When eating bowls of noodles or rice, it is common to lift the bowl up and simply shovel the food into one's mouth instead of trying to contend with individual noodles or grains of rice.

HOW TO HOLD CHOPSTICKS

1. Hold one chopstick between your thumb and middle finger. Position it so that it rests at the base of your thumb (on the joint) and between the tips of your middle and ring fingers. It shouldn't touch the index finger.

2. Place the second chopstick between the thumb and index finger. The side of the chopstick should rest against the tip of your thumb, and the top of the chopstick should rest against the pad of your index finger.

3. Keep the chopsticks parallel. As you grip the food, the first chopstick should be kept still; the second chopstick should move up and down to grip and release.

4. Persist, because practice makes perfect. Try picking up various foods, such as slippery dumplings, clumps of rice, and soft tofu to hone your skills. It may comfort you to know that even adult Chinese people sometimes drop their food onto the table or floor when using chopsticks. When you can pick up and eat a whole chicken leg whilst gripping it with chopsticks, or gracefully turn over a large fish without splashing the sauce, your training can be considered complete.

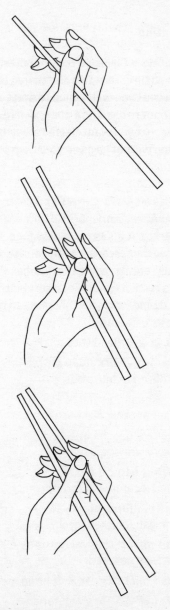

How to hold chopsticks

Communal eating

Remember, eating in China is a communal experience. Dishes will be placed in the middle of the table and shared between all the diners. In most restaurants you will be given a bowl, in which you put the food you are about to eat, and a plate, where you discard bones and everything else that you want cleared away. In most Chinese restaurants, you will not be given your own plate of food.

HELP ORDERING CHINESE FOOD

Clement Atlee, former British Prime Minister, was no stranger to the allure of Chinese food. He famously said 'I just love Chinese food. My favourite dish is number 27.' Naturally, only knowing the number of your favourite dish in a certain restaurant won't help you in China. The following words and phrases can help you order in a Chinese restaurant.

diǎncài 点菜 Order dishes

Qǐng gěi wǒ yīfèn càidān 请给我一份菜单
Could I have a menu, please?

Zài lái yīshuāng kuàizi 再来一双筷子
Can I have another pair of chopsticks?

Qǐng gěi wǒ dàochá 请给我倒茶
Please serve me some tea.

Nǐ tuījiàn jǐ dào cài ba 你推荐几道菜吧
Could you recommend some dishes?

Wǒ yào chī...jīròu/niúròu 我要吃……鸡肉/牛肉
I want to eat...chicken/beef.

lái yīdào dìfāng tèsè cài 来一道地方特色菜
I want a local delicacy.

Lái yīwǎn mǐfàn 来一碗米饭 Bring me a bowl of rice.

Wǒ chī sù 我吃素 I'm a vegetarian.

> *Wǒ bù chī là* 我不吃辣 I don't eat spicy food.
>
> *mǎidān* 买单 Cheque, please.
>
> *Fúwùyuán, tānglǐ yǒu zhī cāngying!* 服务员，汤里有只苍蝇！ Waiter, there's a fly in my soup!
>
> Tipping is not usually practised in China. If you do leave a tip, your waiter may very well come running after you with the money you 'left behind'.

Soup

Soups are a central part of most large Chinese meals. Unlike in the West, where it is customary to have the soup before the main course, the Chinese prefer to eat soup during a meal. The soup dish often acts as the drink – the word for soup, *tāng* is after all the same as the word for 'hot water': *tāng* 汤. It is not out of the ordinary for people to not have a separate drink during dinner, they will instead rely on drinking the soup.

The rice bowls

In Chinese, 'rice bowl' (*fànwǎn* 饭碗) is used metaphorically to refer to one's livelihood – much like the word 'bread' is used in the West. The phrase *qiǎngfànwǎn* 抢饭碗 means 'fight for a job' or 'snatch someone's job'. The best 'rice bowls' are often seen as being jobs in the Chinese civil service, because government jobs are known for their high levels of job security. They are commonly divided into the following categories:

- *jīn fànwǎn* 金饭碗 'gold rice bowl' – job in a central government office
- *yín fànwǎn* 银饭碗 'silver rice bowl' – job in a provincial government office
- *tóng fànwǎn* 铜饭碗 'copper rice bowl' – job in a municipal government office

- *tiě fànwǎn* 铁饭碗 'iron rice bowl' – job in a district or street-level government office
- *ní fànwǎn* 泥饭碗 'clay rice bowl' – private sector work with little to no job security

The civil service examinations are sometimes jokingly referred to as the 'great war of the rice bowls', *zhēngwǎn dàzhàn* 争碗大战.

Chinese medicine and food

One of the oldest tenets of traditional Chinese medicine says that whichever body part of an animal is eaten will help nourish the corresponding part of our own bodies. This is known as *chī shénme, bǔ shénme* 吃什么，补什么 – 'what is eaten, is what is nourished'. Thus some believe that eating liver will help those suffering from liver problems, eating fish eyes will help with your eyesight, and eating duck's tongues can help you speak like a fabulous orator (and not, conversely, like Donald Duck). Don't expect eating fish gills or chicken wings to help you to breathe underwater or fly off into the sunset, however.

Eating the Chinese medicine way

Chinese people like to point out the medicinal properties of various foods (whether real or imagined). The Chinese word for 'take medicine' is *chīyào* 吃药, literally 'eat medicine'. The following is a collection of some of the more commonly desired medicinal effects, together with the foodstuffs associated with them, in the Chinese consciousness. Remember that this advice – not unlike most Chinese cooking – should be taken with a dose of salt.

- Boosting brain function: pumpkin, walnut, egg, seaweed, banana
- Nourishing the kidneys: sesame, cowpea, red bean, sea cucumber
- Nourishing the liver: sticky rice, Chinese sorghum, red jujube, longan

- Strengthening the spleen: lotus seed, astragalus root, Chinese yam, hawthorn
- Strengthening the lungs: pomegranate, sugar cane, water chestnut, lily
- Increasing one's vital energies: soya bean, quail, finless eel, ginseng
- Enriching the blood: donkey-hide glue, pig's blood, pork liver, brown sugar

The geography of Chinese cuisine

If one were asked to give a simplistic breakdown of the flavours of China's cuisine by geographical region, the short answer would be that Chinese food tends to be 'sweet in the south, salty in the north, sour in the east, and spicy in the west'. In South China, where the main crop is paddy rice, it should come as no surprise that the staple food is rice. In the colder north, wheat flour forms the mainstay of the diet.

China is home to 56 ethnicities, but the food of the dominant Han culture is what has come to be known as 'Chinese food' abroad. Some of China's ethnic groups live in harsher climes, less suited to agricultural production. The Tibetans are one example, and their food is not so well-regarded – especially by the sometimes elitist Han people. Take this extract from a Russian traveller's account of Tibetan cuisine, written in the years before World War Two:

> *The yak steaks could not be tackled with knives – only with sharp axes; fried potatoes were raw, and the soup was plainly a dirty dish-water with something indescribable floating in it. In Gardar, in Sikang [Sichuan] Province, I had to exist for two months on a diet prepared by the Tibetan women of the Morowa tribe and, at the end, nearly gave up the ghost.*
>
> **Peter Goullart, Forbidden Kingdom**

This is either mostly exaggeration, bad luck, or a combination of the two, but the fact remains that China's most respected culinary traditions are Han Chinese in origin – albeit with certain ethnic influences. Traditional Chinese cooking can be divided into **eight** major styles. These styles are distinctive from one another due to certain factors that influenced their development, such as climate, geography, history, and lifestyle.

> ### *TĀOTIÈ DÀCĀN* 饕餮大餐
> This idiom is used to describe a great feast, and is the equivalent of the English saying 'a feast fit for a king'. Literally, it means 'a feast fit for Taotie'. In Chinese legend, Taotie is the ferocious and very greedy fifth son of the Dragon King.

Lǔ (Shandong)

Lu cuisine (*Lǔcài* 鲁菜) developed alongside the history and culture of Shandong province. It takes its name from the historic State of Lu (*Lǔguó* 鲁国), the old name for Shandong and the home of Confucius. As early as the Xia Dynasty (c. 2000 BC) people were using salt to flavour their food in this region. Lu cuisine is known for being mild and fresh, using plenty of seafood, such as prawns, shellfish, and abalone. Local delicacies include shark's fin with crab roe (*xièhuáng yúchì* 蟹黄鱼翅), and ' Eight Immortals crossing the sea, teasing the arhats [Buddhist monks]' (*bāxiān guòhǎi nào luóhàn* 八仙过海闹罗汉), which is a starter that includes the eight ingredients of shark's fin, sea cucumber, abalone, fish bones, fish bladder, prawns, asparagus, and ham to represent the Eight Taoist Immortals. More economical, everyday foods in the area are mainly flour-based. Think plenty of noodles, breads, dumplings, and steamed buns. Despite being among the oldest of China's culinary traditions, Shandong cuisine is difficult to find outside Northern China.

Chuān (Sichuan)

Sichuan cuisine (*Chuāncài* 川菜) is one of China's most famous cooking styles – so much so that it can be found in restaurants around the world (sometimes spelled 'Szechuan', or other varieties thereof). Its centre is the provincial capital of Sichuan province, Chengdu, and it's famous for strong, spicy flavours. Chilli peppers, peppercorns, and Sichuan peppers are liberally used to flavour dishes and create such tastes as 'numbing and spicy' (*málà* 麻辣), 'sour and hot' (*suānlà* 酸辣), and even the suspect-sounding but quite delicious 'fish-scented' (*yúxiāng* 鱼香). Sichuan cuisine boasts over 300 dishes, some of which are favourites among foreigners, such as spicy diced chicken (*gōngbào jīdīng* 宫保鸡丁, otherwise known as 'Kung Pao Chicken'). 'Husband and wife lung slices', *fūqī fèipiàn* 夫妻肺片, is another famous Sichuan dish. Despite its off-putting name, actual lungs aren't an ingredient. This cold dish is made from sliced beef, as well as a generous amount of spices and peppercorns, which serve to provide the desired mouth-numbingly spicy flavour. The name comes from a husband and wife who became well-known for selling such beef slices on the streets of Chengdu, capital of Sichuan, in the 1930s.

Yuè (Guangdong)

Yue cuisine (*Yuècài* 粤菜) originated in the southern province of Guangdong (formerly Canton), and since spread to Hong Kong and the rest of the world. When people in the West talk about 'Chinese food', they mostly mean Cantonese or Yue cuisine, thanks to the large number of people who emigrated from Guangdong in the nineteenth and twentieth centuries. People in China say that Cantonese people dare to eat anything – and urban legends of Cantonese people eating human foetuses are widespread. Grisly stories aside, Yue cuisine does feature such exciting delicacies as snake, dog, rat, and even raw monkey's brain. For the less adventurous, Yue cuisine is also the home of *diǎnxīn* 点心 (known as dim sum in Cantonese), which can be found everywhere in China and across many parts of the world.

Dianxin are small bite-sized snacks or individual portions of food, which are traditionally served in small steamer baskets or on small plates. Types of dianxin include steamed buns, dumplings, and spring rolls.

Sū (Jiangsu)

Emerging in the lower regions of the Yangtze River in an area now known as Jiangsu province, Su cuisine (*Sūcài* 苏菜) is well-regarded for its rich, but not greasy, flavours and an emphasis on seasonal produce. Chinese legend tells of how the imperial cook, Yi Ya, once travelled to Xuzhou in Jiangsu to teach the locals how to cook. There he developed a dish which was known as 'mutton concealed in the belly of the fish', *yúfù cáng yángròu* 鱼腹藏羊肉, which was a mouth-watering combination of lamb and fish. It is said that the character *xiān* 鲜, meaning 'fresh and tasty', comes from this dish – the character is a combination of *yú* 鱼, 'fish', and *yáng* 羊, 'lamb'. One of Su cuisine's most simple and widespread dishes is Yangzhou fried rice (*Yángzhōu chǎofàn* 扬州炒饭). It is made by frying rice with a variety of ingredients, including egg, ham, chicken, peas, and sweetcorn.

Mǐn (Fujian)

Min cuisine (*Mǐncài* 闽菜) is the culinary tradition of Fujian province – 'Min' being the shorthand for that region. As Fujian is a coastal province, Min cuisine features a diverse range of seafood, including hundreds of types of fish, shellfish, and turtles. Fujian cuisine attaches special importance to the brewing of all kinds of soup, from thin seafood soups to thicker Fujian *gēng* 羹. Cutting and slicing techniques are highly-valued in Fujian, and chefs from the region are said to be able to cut meat and vegetables into strips 'as fine as hair', and slices 'as thin as a paper'. The region is home to a type of clam that looks like a human tongue, and people call it 'the tongue of Xishi' (*Xīshīshé* 西施舌) after the legendary Chinese beauty who drowned in a river.

Huī (Anhui)

Anhui cuisine (*Huīcài* 徽菜) is mostly derived from the native cooking styles of the area that surrounds the Yellow Mountain. It is similar to Jiangsu cuisine, but with less emphasis on seafood (being a landlocked province), and more on a wide variety of local herbs and vegetables. Anhui province is known for its bamboo forests, and fresh bamboo and mushroom crops feature heavily in the cuisine of the region. Certain foods, such as bamboo shoots, are eaten primarily for their texture and not their flavour. The Chinese like to feel the supple give of the bamboo on their teeth as they chew.

Zhè (Zhejiang)

Zhe cuisine (*Zhècài* 浙菜), which originated in the eastern coastal province of Zhejiang, is categorized by its delicate flavours and mellow aromas. Dragon Well prawns (*Lóngjǐng xiārén* 龙井虾仁) is one of the region's more representative dishes, using a combination of aromatic Dragon Well tea leaves, grown in the tea fields surrounding scenic West Lake in provincial capital Hangzhou, and freshly peeled prawns.

Xiāng (Hunan)

The central province of Hunan is home to Xiang cuisine (*Xiāngcài* 湘菜), with its strong, aromatic oils and liberal use of spice. While Sichuanese food is often considered to be the centre of spicy, hot cuisine in China, Xiang cuisine is famous for being even spicier. There is a popular saying that goes: *Jiāngxīrén búpà là, Sìchuānrén là búpà, Húnánrén pà búlà* 江西人不怕辣，四川人辣不怕，湖南人怕不辣, which roughly means 'while people from Jiangxi and Sichuan aren't afraid of spicy food, people from Hunan are afraid of food that **isn't** spicy'. A popular dish is *duòjiāo yútóu* 剁椒鱼头, 'steamed fish head with diced hot peppers'. The head of a fish is considered to contain the tenderest, most flavoursome meat.

Street food

Travellers and local residents alike swear by China's street food, claiming that it is among the most 'real' and authentic types of Chinese cuisine. While it's undoubtedly true that street food is generally oily and unhealthy – the oil used to fry a lot of it is rarely fresh – street food offers a communal, lively, and most of all cheap, eating experience. Broadly speaking, street food can consist of anything that is sold from carts and stalls on the street, and is consequently quick and highly convenient. It normally falls into several identifiable categories:

clockwise from top left – bing, barbecue kebab, dumpling,
numb and spicy soup

Barbecue *shāokǎo* 烧烤

Barbecue stalls are generally just small charcoal grills, on which anything from meat skewers to squid and whole aubergines are barbecued, along with plenty of spices. *Yángròuchuàn* 羊肉串, lamb kebabs, which originate from the far-western province of Xinjiang, are a particular favourite.

Numb and spicy soup *málàtàng* 麻辣烫

This spicy do-it-yourself soup, so common in China, is actually quite similar to a hot pot. The ingredients are mostly skewered on thin sticks, and boiled in a pre-prepared broth. Patrons first take a plastic basket, and fill it with all manner of different raw ingredients, such as mushrooms, chicken wings, chicken cartilage, tofu, and pork balls. The ingredients are then handed over to the server, who will boil them in a spicy soup.

Bǐng 饼

The Chinese *bǐng* is a word used to describe all kinds of wheat flour-based breads and cakes – if it's flat and round, the chances are that it's a *bǐng*. If someone is said to have a *bǐngliǎn* 饼脸, 'flat bread face', then they are considered to have flat facial features. Common types of bing are the *shāobǐng* 烧饼, a baked pancake covered in sesame seeds, and the *jiānbǐng* 煎饼, a fried pancake which is a popular breakfast food that can be prepared with a variety of ingredients, such as egg, ham, and spring onions.

Dumplings *shuǐjiǎo* 水饺

Dumplings are not only one of China's most common dishes, but also a highly symbolic food. In Northern China, there is a saying: 'dumplings for a journey, noodles for a homecoming' (*chūmén jiǎozi, jìnmén miàn* 出门饺子，进门面). This essentially means that dumplings are a traditional sending-off meal for people going away on a trip, and noodles are customarily eaten when people return home. Dumplings are said to represent the togetherness of a family, while noodles can be thought of as symbolizing 'ropes' that connect people – 'the ties that bind'.

Dumplings are made by rolling flat a small piece of dough, and putting the ground meat and vegetable filling inside. The dough is then sealed by pressing the edges together, so that they look a bit like the gold or silver ingots, *yuánbǎo* 元宝, that were used as currency in ancient China. Making dumplings is a family activity in which all generations can take part – the person who makes the nicest looking dumplings will be praised, while those who make ugly, irregular dumplings will be mocked, albeit all in good fun. Poorly made dumplings will break apart when they are boiled.

> **THE FIVE FLAVOURS** *WǓWÈI* 五味
> Traditional Chinese medicine dictates that there are 'five' different kinds of flavour: sweet (*tián* 甜), sour (*suān* 酸), bitter (*kǔ* 苦), spicy (*là* 辣), and salty (*xián* 咸).

Tea

In China, tea is a way of life. It is close to a religion – China even has a 'tea saint', Lu Yu 陆羽, who wrote a holy scripture all about the drink – *The Classic of Tea* (*Chájīng* 《茶经》). This work was written in the Tang dynasty, and roughly marks the period when tea ceased to be just a drink, and became an important part of the Chinese cultural heritage. In the West we like to say 'an apple a day keeps the doctor away'. In China they have a similar saying from the Tang dynasty that swaps apples for tea: 'one day without tea will bring illness'. Today, people from all walks of life carry flasks of tea that are topped up with hot water at regular intervals, and bottled tea drinks are a major industry. The first thing that any visitor or guest will be offered after they sit down is a cup of Chinese tea. When drinking tea from a small cup, it is preferable to finish in three sips. The first is for tasting the tea, the second is drinking, and the third is for savouring. Fittingly, the Chinese character for 'savour', *pǐn* is 品 – composed of three mouths (*kǒu* 口).

> **DID YOU KNOW?**
> The English words 'tea' and 'cha' derive from different regional pronunciations of the Chinese character for tea – *chá* 茶. While 'cha' comes from the *cha* of the northern Mandarin dialect, 'tea' comes from tê, the Hokkien dialect spoken in Fujian province.

The discovery of tea is often attributed to the legendary ruler of China, Shennong 神农, who lived some 5,000 years ago. He is said to have been the first to discover the medicinal uses of herbs. He did this by blindly tasting a hundred different plants, of which he declared 72 to be poisonous. After ingesting so much poison, he found that tea from the plant *Camellia sinensis* acted as an antidote. Tea started out life as a medicine. Regarding the medicinal functions of tea, Chinese people, both ancient and modern, agree on several: it can improve the vision, act as an expectorant, and dispel drowsiness, just to name a few. Grander claims, such as its ability to prevent cancer, have also been made.

Tea has long been associated with Buddhism, and can often be found growing in monastery gardens. Tea has three very strong points as far as practising Buddhism is concerned: during meditation it uplifts the spirits, it aids digestion, and doesn't lead to thoughts of the opposite sex. In this way tea walked from the common household through the Buddha's gate.

THE ANCIENT TEA HORSE ROAD *CHÁMǍ GǓDÀO* 茶马古道

This ancient trade route stretches from the town of Pu'er in Southern Yunnan province to Lhasa in Tibet, and beyond into India. Mostly used to transport tea, it was probably China's second most important overland trade route after the Silk Road. At some points the mountainous path becomes so narrow and treacherous that when caravans travelling in opposite directions met head-on, one party would have had no choice but to fling their precious cargo down the mountain.

Types of tea

Green tea (*lǜchá* 绿茶) is the most widely-consumed variety of tea in China. It is also the freshest kind of tea – newly-picked leaves are heated and dried, but not fermented. This helps the leaves to retain their original colour. A popular variety is *Lóngjǐng* 龙井, or 'Dragon Well' tea, which is grown in Zhejiang province, and was declared by Qing emperor Kangxi to be fit for use as an official imperial tribute. Longjing picked in early spring, before the Qingming Festival, is highly prized, as the shoots are most tender during this period.

In China, black tea is known as 'red tea' – *hóngchá* 红茶 – due to the colour of the liquid. Black tea leaves are fully fermented, which gives them a strong flavour. This is the favoured tea of the Western world.

Oolong tea (*wūlóngchá* 乌龙茶) leaves are partially fermented, half-way between fresh green tea leaves and the fully fermented leaves of black tea. Oolong tea leaves can be recognized by their unique colouring – green in the centre, and reddish-brown around the edges. Oolong tea has a strong, long-lasting flavour – leaves of

Anhui *tiěguānyīn* 铁观音 can be steeped seven times and still retain their taste.

Pu'er tea (*Pǔ'ěrchá* 普洱茶) is fully fermented black tea that has usually been aged. This gives it a full, musky flavour that is highly prized among connoisseurs. Pu'er comes from the Pu'er region of Yunnan province, and is often sold compressed into 'tea bricks'.

Wine

China has been making alcohol, *jiǔ* 酒, for millennia. The *Records of the Grand Historian* narrates the legend of the despotic King Zhou of the Shang dynasty, who stockpiled 'forests of hanging meat and pools of wine' in his palace while the populace starved. Alcohol has long been ingrained into all aspects of Chinese society, and roughly one fifth of all Tang poetry has wine as its subject. The Chinese have placed a great emphasis on ceremony since time immemorial. At gatherings, celebrations, and rituals, alcohol has always been of utmost importance. Being fond of drink is not as negative a characteristic in China as in the West. There are in fact two words for 'alcoholic' in Chinese: the derogatory *jiǔguǐ* 酒鬼, literally 'alcohol fiend', and the honorific *jiǔxiān* 酒仙, literally 'alcohol divinity'. The latter was one of the nicknames of Tang poet Li Bai, who was well-known for his love of alcohol.

The Chinese traditionally drink *báijiǔ* 白酒, a clear spirit usually distilled from sorghum or maize, that has an alcohol content of between 40 per cent and 60 per cent. Some have claimed that *báijiǔ* is the world's most popular spirit, but to many non-Chinese its high alcohol content can cause it be compared to paint thinner, or worse. Yellow wine (*huángjiǔ* 黄酒) is a type of alcohol that is brewed from grains such as rice, millet, or wheat. Because it is not distilled, yellow wine tends to have an alcohol content of less than 20 per cent.

DID YOU KNOW?

According to Chinese etiquette, when filling someone's tea cup, it should be filled to seven tenths of its capacity. When pouring a wine or other alcoholic drink, the glass should be filled to eight tenths of its capacity. This is known as *chá qī jiǔ bā* 茶七酒八, literally 'tea seven, wine eight'.

Chapter 12:
Art and culture
艺术与文化
yìshù yǔ wénhuà

Art and culture
艺术与文化

yìshù yǔ wénhuà

> *First we look at the hills in the painting,*
> *Then we look at the painting in the hills.*
> **Li Yu, Qing dynasty playwright**

China is not the most ancient of the world's civilizations, but it is the oldest continuous culture that still exists today. The Chinese are themselves equal parts proud, equal parts in awe of their own cultural inheritance, frequently describing it as *bódà jīngshēn* 博大精深, 'extensive and profound'. This can often feel like an understatement. If a great calligrapher can dedicate a whole year to the writing of a single Chinese character, and still not master it; if a great artist can dedicate his life to the painting of a single node of bamboo, and not capture its spirit, then what are we to do? We can only hope to scratch the surface when it comes to gaining an appreciation of Chinese culture as a whole.

That 'nature and humanity are one' (*tiān rén hé yī* 天人合一) is a concept that the Chinese practically have a copyright on. Much of China's traditional art and culture is based on this ideal – that man and nature should come together as one. This goes some way to explaining the natural, flowing shapes found in China's writing and architecture, and the obsession with mountains and rivers in its paintings. The ethics and virtues of Confucianism are seen as a part of our innate nature, and the path of Taoism is one of seeking unity with the universe. This is the undercurrent that flows within Chinese art, and all of its culture.

Philosophy

Confucius

No single man has influenced China and its culture more than the philosopher Confucius, *Kǒngzǐ* 孔子, (551–478 BC). In recent years, schools dedicated to the teaching of Chinese language and culture, known as 'Confucius institutes', have sprung up in countries all over the world, like bamboo shoots after a spring rain. Even thousands of years after his time, Confucius is still the greatest of China's cultural ambassadors.

His teachings were developed into the system of Confucianism. The Chinese word for 'Confucianism' doesn't contain the name 'Confucius' – it is instead known as *rújiào* 儒教. Here the '*rú*' means 'scholar', while *jiào* is 'teachings', so *rújiào* literally means 'the school of the scholars'. From this we can get a glimpse of the importance of studying and book-learning in Chinese culture.

While the culturally-minded tourist will discover temples dedicated to Confucius in all corners of China, Confucianism as an ideology does not have a belief in the spiritual. There is no supernatural being at its centre; it is instead a value system very much grounded in reality.

The Confucian philosophies of filial piety (*xiàojìng* 孝敬) and ancestor worship still inform a lot of modern Chinese life. Elderly relatives are looked after and cared for by their families wherever possible, not packed off to nursing homes. Children make the effort to return home to see their parents and spend time with them whenever they can, and whole families gather to venerate their forebears at Qingming Festival each year.

Confucius himself was something of a polymath. Aside from his philosophical writings, he is known for compiling a history of the Spring and Autumn Period (the *Spring and Autumn Annals*,

Chūnqiū 春秋), a dictionary-encyclopaedia (*Ěryǎ* 尔雅), and a collection of classical poetry (the *Book of Odes*, *Shījīng* 诗经). His writing style was known for being subtly judgemental, and this technique of writing is called *chūnqiū bǐfǎ* 春秋笔法, the 'Spring and Autumn writing technique'. Confucius' birthplace is the town of Qufu in modern-day Shandong province. Qufu has a thriving tourist industry, mostly thanks to the Confucius Temple, which is China's second largest complex of historical buildings after the Forbidden City in Beijing.

DID YOU KNOW?
Influential thinkers in China were often given honorific titles ending in *zǐ* 子, meaning 'master'. Thus Confucius is known in Chinese as 'Master Kong' (*Kǒngzǐ* 孔子), and Mencius is 'Master Meng' (*Mèngzǐ* 孟子).

The ideology of Confucianism focuses on the cultivation of virtue and the upholding of high moral standards. One of its main ideals is to strive to become a 'gentleman' or 'perfect man', *jūnzǐ* in Chinese. The junzi is someone who combines the morality of a saint, the intelligence and drive of a scholar, and the social mores of a gentleman.

These 'gentlemen' were expected to act as a moral compass for society as a whole. As a popular saying goes, *jūnzǐ dòngkǒu bú dòngshǒu* 君子动口不动手, 'the gentleman fights with his words, not with his fists'. The polar opposite of the gentleman is the *xiǎorén* 小人, literally 'small person', people who are petty and small-minded. Conventional Confucian wisdom tells us to avoid selfish, petty desires in our dealings with others, warning us against 'measuring the stature of great men by the yardstick of small men', *yǐ xiǎorén zhī xīn duó jūnzǐ zhī fù* 以小人之心度君子之腹.

Mencius

The man of second most importance in the Confucian tradition is probably Mencius, *Mèngzǐ* 孟子, (372–289 BC). Like Confucius, he was a wandering philosopher, who travelled around China's feudal kingdoms offering sound moral and political advice to their rulers. A shining example of the virtue of filial piety, Mencius took three years away from his official duties to mourn the passing of his mother.

> *MÈNGMǓ SĀNQIĀN* 孟母三迁 **MENCIUS' MOTHER MOVES THREE TIMES**
> Mencius' mother is one of China's most revered female figures. When Mencius was just a child, she uprooted the family and moved house three times before finding an ideal location to bring up her son. Her perseverance paid off, and Mencius grew up to be one of China's most important philosophers. Nowadays the idiom is used to refer to the importance of finding a suitable environment for raising one's children.

Mencius believed that people are good by nature, and that it is external factors, such as the influence of society, that causes people's moral character to change. This is most famously expressed in the phrase '*Rén zhī chū, xìng běn shàn, xìng xiāng jìn, xí xiāng yuǎn.* 人之初，性本善，性相近，习相远', which can be rendered as 'At their birth, men are naturally good. Their natures are much the same; their habits become widely different.'

Laozi

The semi-mythical Chinese philosopher Laozi (*Lǎozǐ* 老子, sometimes written in English as 'Lao Tzu'), who lived in the sixth century BC, is seen as the father of the only religion native to China – Taoism.

If Confucianism is an example of a firmly grounded, practical belief system, then Taoism is its polar opposite. Taoists try to reach harmony with the Tao, or *Dào* 道, which is sometimes explained as the 'way of all things'. Laozi is the reputed author of Taoism's founding scripture, the *Dàodéjīng* 《道德经》, *The Classic of the Way and the Power*. Laozi was later venerated as a God by Taoist believers. Some see Taoism as a path that leads toward immortality, and historical Taoists were primarily concerned with finding the secret of eternal life. Qin Shi Huang, the first Emperor of China, is said to have died from mercury poisoning. He was following the advice of a Taoist priest, who, quite ironically, told him that ingesting the mercury would help him to live forever. Laozi was the first of China's recluses. According to myth, he renounced public life at the ripe old age of 160 and travelled to the western wilderness atop a water buffalo, never to be heard from again.

'Laozi' was not his real name, and is more of an honorific title. The *lǎo* means 'old', and the 'zi' is an honorific suffix meaning 'master'. Laozi's real family name was probably *Lǐ* 李, and his given name was *ěr* 耳, which means 'ear'. The ruling family of the Tang dynasty was also surnamed *Lǐ* 李, and they traced their lineage back to Laozi himself. He was given the posthumous name *Dān* 聃, which means 'long ears', and Laozi is normally portrayed as an old man with very long earlobes. To this day, long, fleshy earlobes are seen as a mark of good fortune in China.

Zhuangzi

Zhuangzi 庄子 is a fourth century BC Taoist philosopher who reputedly authored the work that bears his name, the *Zhuāngzǐ* 《庄子》. This is considered the second most important text in the Taoist tradition, after the *Dàodéjīng* 《道德经》. While Confucius stressed the importance of adhering to a strict system of social conduct, Zhuangzi is known for advocating a philosophy based upon freedom and spontaneity, away from the pressures of social life.

One of the most well-known passages in the *Zhuāngzǐ* is the 'butterfly dream'. This passage recounts the time when Zhuangzi dreamt that he was a butterfly, fluttering around freely in the air. He didn't know that he was Zhuangzi, all he knew was that he was just a simple butterfly. When he awoke, he recalled that he was Zhuangzi – but he didn't know if he was the Zhuangzi that had dreamt of being a butterfly, or a butterfly, dreaming that he was Zhuangzi.

Zhuangzi's butterfly dream

Chinese kung fu

The worldwide popularity of Hong Kong kung fu cinema has led many to believe that almost all Chinese people are good at kung fu. To a very limited extent, this is true: most Chinese people do learn some kung fu at school or university, and anyone who takes an early morning stroll around a Chinese park will see groups of retirees practising Tai chi.

These days, the word 'kung fu' (*gōngfu* 功夫) is not just limited to one's martial arts ability. It can simply be used to refer to one's skill at performing any particular task, from using spreadsheet software to cooking pasta.

Chinese kung fu is not just a martial art or a simple form of exercise, it is a crystallization of traditional Chinese culture. Chinese kung fu, at its heart, shares ideals with Confucianism, in that it is about cultivating moral character, and Taoism, in its emphasis on seeking inner peace.

The earliest origins of Chinese martial arts have been traced back to prehistoric hunting techniques and military training in ancient China. Soldiers were trained in hand-to-hand combat as early as the first Chinese dynasty, the Xia, some 4,000 years ago. It wasn't until much later however, during the Ming and Qing dynasties, that martial arts became clearly divided into different schools.

The Chinese martial arts can be divided into two distinct schools, the *nèijiā* 内家, 'internal school', which is more concerned with the spiritual and mental side of martial practice, and the *wàijiā* 外家, or 'external school', which is more focused on the physiological aspects of kung fu. While internal martial arts are generally performed at a slower pace, helping to improve concentration and coordination, external styles are more explosive, with an emphasis on muscular power.

The romantic ideal of the warrior monk, and no doubt the canny business acumen of recent abbots, has helped Shaolin kung fu (*Shàolín gōngfu* 少林功夫) become China's most famous school of martial arts. Shaolin kung fu, a famously external style, originated in the Shaolin Monastery, Henan province. It is said that the Indian monk, Bodhidarma, came to the temple in the year 527 AD. There he sat in front of a wall, meditating in silence for nine years. In the story, Bodhidarma created the techniques of Shaolin kung fu to help toughen his disciples up, preparing them for long spells of meditation, and to help defend the monastery in times of need.

Just as Shaolin kung fu has its roots in Buddhist legend, Tai chi (*tàijí* 太极) is inseparable from Taoist myth. The Taoist monk Zhang Sanfeng is traditionally credited with creating the internal style of Tai chi in the twelfth century. A semi-mythical figure, Zhang Sanfeng is sometimes depicted as being seven feet tall, and many sources claim that he lived to be 212 years old. He is often associated with the Taoist monasteries of Wudang Mountain in Hebei province.

Art

The 'true' Chinese artist, at least of the pre-modern world, is a man at peace with nature, someone whose spirit dwells in the mountains and rivers, untouched by temptations of gold and riches. The Chinese also believed that a good artist should be a good man – a Confucian *jūnzǐ* – and that a person's ethics and morality were revealed in their artistic work. Traditional Chinese painting is primarily concerned with the natural world. Famous painters throughout history would travel to broaden their minds, with some even spending years living in seclusion, attuning themselves to the rhythms of nature. Traditional Chinese painting, known today as *guóhuà* 国画, 'national painting', is mostly concerned with landscapes. In Chinese, landscape painting is called *shānshuǐ* 山水, literally 'mountains and rivers', after its most favoured subjects.

> **DID YOU KNOW?**
> Chinese painters were particularly fond of painting the 'four gentlemen' (*sìjūnzǐ* 四君子), namely: plum blossoms, orchids, bamboo and chrysanthemums.

The great Chinese painters were usually great calligraphers too. They would equate forms in nature with calligraphy strokes – as the strokes of the characters themselves derived from primitive pictures or pictographs. There are many stories of artists finding inspiration in nature. It is said that the Tang dynasty calligrapher-monk Huai Su 怀素 spent an evening listening to the roar of the Jialing river, and that the resulting inspiration greatly helped his cursive script. Northern Song painter Wen Tong 文同 on the other hand was moved to greater artistic heights simply by the sight of two snakes fighting on the ground. Painting and calligraphy are also closely related to poetry. By the Yuan dynasty, painters combined all three arts. Poems were written in beautiful script on the same canvas as a painting, as a companion piece to the artwork.

> **THE FOUR ARTS OF THE CHINESE SCHOLAR**
> *QÍN QÍ SHŪ HUÀ* 琴棋书画
> In ancient China, to be considered a real scholar, one had to be proficient in all four of the 'scholarly arts': the zither, the game of Go, calligraphy, and painting. The Chinese zither (*qín* 琴), known as the instrument of the sages, is a plucked instrument with seven strings. Chinese legend has it that it was invented over 4,000 years ago, and Confucius himself was said to have used the qin as a means of educating his students. In Chinese, the game of Go is known as *Wéiqí* 围棋, which means 'encirclement game'. Some say it was developed by ancient Chinese chieftains, who would place stones to map out military strategies.

Classic literature

If you take a cursory glance at any Chinese bookshelf, you're likely to find a copy of at least one of the Four Great Classical Novels (*sì dà míngzhù* 四大名著). These four books are considered to be the high watermark of Chinese literature.

The novels, written during the Ming and Qing dynasties, are all instantly familiar to most Chinese people today. Even if they haven't read the original works, people who were brought up in China will have seen the television dramas and film adaptations, played the computer games, or read the comic books.

Romance of the Three Kingdoms

The *Romance of the Three Kingdoms* (*Sānguó Yǎnyì* 三国演义), written by Luo Guanzhong (1330–1400 AD), was China's first full length novel, and is probably China's most widely-read work of historical fiction. The novel relates the political struggles of the Three Kingdoms of Wei, Shu, and Wu in the period between the end of the Eastern Han dynasty (25–220 AD) and the beginning of the Western Jin dynasty (265–316 AD). Luo based his story on oral traditions that had been passed down by storytellers from generation to generation, as well as actual historical records.

The opening words of the novel reflect what is still a common Chinese world-view: 'a kingdom once divided must become united, a kingdom once united must divide.' The Three Kingdoms is a cultural touchstone, and has significantly shaped popular attitudes toward the historical figures that play the heroes and villains. The politician and warlord Cao Cao 曹操, the novel's primary antagonist, is now generally reviled as a treacherous and cunning man, while historical evidence shows him as a capable, well-meaning ruler. Today the Chinese equivalent of the English saying 'speak of the devil' is '*shuō Cáo Cāo, Cáo Cāo dào* 说曹操，曹操到', literally 'Speak of Cao Cao and Cao Cao arrives'.

A wealth of military stratagems are used in the battles that take place throughout the story, and some have entered the modern vernacular. One of these is the 'empty city strategy', *kōngchéng jì* 空城计, a ploy devised by strategist Zhuge Liang to defend a city from an approaching army with only a handful of troops. Zhuge Liang ordered the city gates to be cast wide open, and instructed his soldiers, disguised as civilians, to sweep the roads while he sat on the viewing platform above the gates. There he played his Chinese zither, looking for all the world like there was not a care on his mind. When the enemy commander arrived with his army in tow, he was surprised to see Zhuge Liang so unmoved by the threat that he posed. Suspecting that there was an ambush awaiting them inside the city, he ordered a retreat. Today, the 'empty city strategy', or *kōngchéngjì*, is used to mean 'putting on a bold front to conceal a weakness'.

Dream of the Red Chamber

Dream of the Red Chamber, *Hóng Lóu Mèng* 红楼梦, is a novel that charts the rise and fall of the aristocratic Jia family in Qing dynasty China. The 'red chamber' from the title probably refers to the woman's chambers of a traditional Chinese household. It is part novel of manners, part metaphysical commentary on the nature of life. It is ranked as the first among the four great classical novels, and some say it is China's most important novel. There is even a branch of academic studies, known as *Hóngxué* 红学 ('Redology'), that is devoted to researching every aspect of the life and work of its author, Cao Xueqin 曹雪芹 (1715–1763).

To some degree, the events of the story mirror the fortunes of the author's own life – the fictional Jia family, like Cao's own family, fall into poverty and disgrace. The manuscript was unfinished at the time of Cao's death, and the ending as it stands today was allegedly penned by his friend, Gao E. Some of the characters have entered China's popular consciousness. One of the female protagonists, Lin Daiyu 林黛玉, who is perhaps China's most studied female literary figure, is described as having a naturally weak constitution. Today people use the name Lin Daiyu, or just 'little sister Lin' (*Lín mèimei* 林妹妹) to refer to someone who has a poor constitution.

Journey to the West

The Ming dynasty novel *Journey to the West*, *Xī Yóu Jì* 《西游记》, is, if not the most well written of the four great novels, at least one of the most widely loved. Its protagonist is one of China's most distinctive cultural icons – the Monkey King, a talking monkey with supernatural Taoist powers. The novel is a fictional re-telling of the seventh century spiritual pilgrimage from China to India made by Buddhist monk Xuanzang. The story is episodic and quite repetitive in nature, but children love the imaginative depictions of various monsters and demons, as well as the comedic nature of the Monkey King and his sidekicks, Pigsy the talking pig demon, and Sandy the sand demon. Both were heavenly immortals, sent down to earth to atone for their sins.

At the beginning of the novel, the Monkey King rebels against the forces of Heaven, before being trapped under a mountain by the Buddha. The Chinese expression *dà nào tiāngōng* 大闹天宫, which means 'creating havoc in heaven', is today used to describe someone (usually a child) losing their temper and creating a fuss.

INCANTATION OF THE GOLDEN CIRCLET
JǏNGŪZHÒU 紧箍咒

In the *Journey to the West*, the Monkey King was forced to wear a golden circlet around his head, which could be expanded or contracted by an incantation spoken by the monk, Xuanzang. The monk was thus able to stop the Monkey King from doing anything bad by tightening the circlet and causing him great pain. The word *jǐngūzhòu* can be used to refer to anything that is restrictive in nature, like tight trousers or strict deadlines.

*The main characters of the Journey to the West (from left to right):
the Monkey King, Xuanzang, Pigsy and Sandy*

Water Margin

The Water Margin, *Shuǐ Hǔ Zhuàn* 水浒传, penned in the early days
of the Ming dynasty, was one of the first novels to be written in
vernacular Chinese, and not in the literary Chinese customary at the
time. It is also the first novel to glamourize a peasant uprising, and as
such has been banned at various points in China's history. Its heroes
are the 108 outlaws who are forced into hiding by the corrupt Song
dynasty government. The outlaws are portrayed as just and righteous,
stealing from the rich and giving to the poor, like a Chinese version of
Sherwood Forest's 'Merry Men'.

BĪSHÀNG LIÁNGSHĀN 逼上梁山
Literally 'driven to join the Liangshan mountain [rebels]', this chengyu recalls the story of Lin Chong, who was framed for attempting to assassinate a grand marshal, and subsequently exiled. Lin Chong then joins forces with the Liangshan rebels, the heroes of the novel. Today *bīshàng Liángshān* is used as a phrase meaning 'forced into desperate action'.

Architecture

Away from its distinctive regional capitals, and metropolises like Shanghai and Beijing, China's smaller towns are almost identical replicas of one another. New buildings have sprung up over the course of the past few decades, often replacing older, historic structures. They have become true concrete jungles, all function with no form. Of course, traditional Chinese architecture has survived, but one has to know where to look. At its most simplistic level, Chinese architecture tries to capture nature and imitate its irregularity. The curved rooftops of traditional Chinese house are perhaps the best reflection of this, bringing to mind the bending lines of Chinese calligraphy. The roof is very much the focal point of the Chinese building.

Examples of Chinese architecture

Wells

Water wells (*jǐng* 井) are one of the earliest solutions to one of man's most basic needs: fresh water. They are a testament to China's history, yet are gradually disappearing from China's cities. The traditional *hútòng* 胡同 alleyways of Beijing reveal their importance: the word, *hútòng*, actually originates from the time the Mongols ruled China.

The Mongolian word 'hot-tog' means 'water well', and when people began to settle in an area, they would first dig a well, building their dwellings around it. A well in the Forbidden City is said to be haunted by the ghost of the Guangxu Emperor's favourite concubine, Zhenfei 珍妃, who was thrown down it by the Empress Dowager.

Archways

Páifāng 牌坊 are traditional Chinese gates, which are usually erected either in front of a tomb, temple, ancestral hall, or across a road. The majority of Chinese archways consist of four pillars and three apertures, while grandiose *páifāng* with six pillars and five apertures can only be erected on the site of an imperial tomb. *Páifāng* can be divided into different types according to their function: symbolic archways that signify an important temple or palace; entrance archways that serve to mark the main gateway to a settlement or place; and memorial archways used to honour the

archway

memory of someone who committed great deeds, or to honour a woman's loyalty to her husband. In the past, the construction of a *páifāng* was a very solemn and ceremonious event. They are often used to mark the main thoroughfares of Chinatown areas in cities around the world.

Screen walls

Screen walls (*yǐngbì* 影壁) are isolated walls, found either outside or just inside the main gate of a traditional Chinese building. The majority of screen walls are located opposite the main gate. Those that are placed outside serve to create an outer courtyard together with the decorated archways either side of the door. Inside the main gate, they act as a means of blocking one's line of sight, stopping Peeping Toms from looking into the house. These walls create an

screen wall

illusion of seclusion, and give visitors an extra moment to adjust their clothing once inside the threshold. Such screen walls are a common feature of courtyard-style houses in Northern China.

Pavilions

Pavilions (*tíng* 亭), both ancient and modern, can be found almost everywhere in China – in parks and gardens, atop cloudy mountain peaks, or in busy city centres. The Chinese word for pavilion, *tíng* 亭, comes from the word 'to stop', *tíng* 停, because they are places where footsore passers-by can stop to have a rest. They were originally used for administrative purposes, as wayside kiosks for weary travellers, or as small post houses. Later, they came to be used for decorative purposes in landscaped gardens, and as places in which to simply relax and enjoy one's surroundings.

pavilion

Pagodas

Pagodas (*tǎ* 塔) entered China alongside the spread of Buddhism in the Han dynasty. Early Chinese Buddhists built wooden pagodas that were like the Indian stupas, buildings not for going inside but for the preservation of sacred relics and books. Later Chinese pagodas borrowed Chinese architectural features, such as curved eaves, and were constructed out of stone or brick. The thirteen-storey 'iron pagoda' of Kaifeng was originally a wooden pagoda, built during the Song Dynasty. It burned down during a storm, and was rebuilt with red bricks, which is how it gets its name. China has around 10,000 historic pagodas, more than any other country.

GUIDE TO A TYPICAL CHINESE BUDDHIST TEMPLE

It's possible for tourists to get very tired of temples very quickly in China – after all, Buddhist temples can be found practically everywhere, and tend to be much alike in nature. Some people simply wander aimlessly around the buildings without any knowledge of what they are looking at. However, even the most basic understanding of the layout of a temple can really help one to get the most out of a visit.

China's Buddhist temples more closely resemble its imperial palaces than anything else. They are comprised of two main elements: halls and courtyards. Generally speaking, average-sized temples have three halls separated by two courtyards. Temples, like other important Chinese buildings adhering to the principles of fengshui, normally face south. Before the first hall is the forecourt. This is where one can find the bell that calls the monks to prayer – or dinner.

Upon entering the first hall, one is generally greeted by the affable Maitreya Buddha, known to the Chinese as the 'Laughing Buddha' (*Mílèfó* 弥勒佛). He is flanked by

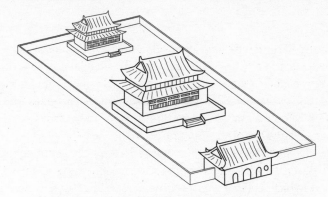

Chinese Buddhist temple, showing the traditional layout of three halls and two courtyards

the Four Heavenly Kings, the Guardians of the Four Directions, after which the hall is named: *Sì Tiānwáng Diàn* 四天王殿 (the Hall of the Four Heavenly Kings). The second hall, otherwise known as the Great Hall, is usually elevated on marble balustrades. Inside, one can find the temple's main altar. Upon it rests the image of Sakyamuni Buddha and his two foremost disciples, Mahakasyapa and Ananda, or other Buddhas from ages past. A large incense burner, or *dǐng* 鼎, is situated before the Great Hall, providing a place for worshippers to burn incense.

The third and rearmost hall is usually divided into several smaller halls or rooms that serve more functional purposes, such as teaching or meditation areas, and perhaps a library. Behind these main buildings one can find the living quarters of the monks, the dining area, and the kitchen. Chinese doorways – especially those leading into temple halls – usually have a high threshold that one has to step over in order to enter. The highest thresholds are reserved for halls honouring the most venerated Buddhas. It is considered extremely disrespectful to step directly onto a threshold.

Laughing Buddha

Fengshui

The ancient Chinese art of *fēngshuǐ* 风水, literally 'wind water', is all about orienting buildings in such a way as to balance the forces of heaven and earth, generating positive 'qi'. Such balance is said to bring about good fortune and improve one's life. Fengshui is divided into two separate branches: fengshui for the tomb (*yīnzhái* 阴宅), and fengshui for the home (*yángzhái* 阳宅).

Belief in fengshui was discouraged after the Communist party came to power, and practitioners were persecuted during the events of the Cultural Revolution. The official attitude toward fengshui has relaxed in recent years, but the teaching and study of the art is still something of a taboo. The modern party line on fengshui is that it is 'part science, part superstition'.

Some general principles of fengshui:

- The most fundamental principle is that houses should be situated 'at the foot of a hill and beside running water' – *yīshān bàngshuǐ* 依山傍水. The Chinese believe that mountains and hills make up the framework of the earth, and water is the source of all life.
- Buildings should be constructed in areas that 'generate qi'. Only in places with a good flow of qi can plants grow strong and humans live long, fruitful lives.
- Buildings should be oriented on a north-south axis, *zuòběi cháonán* 坐北朝南. That is, the rear of a building should face north, and the front should be south-facing. This allows the residence to enjoy the maximum amount of sunshine.

China's capital, Beijing, is constructed in a symmetrical pattern with the Forbidden City at its centre. The Chinese attribute its continued importance and prosperity to its naturally excellent fengshui. To the west of the city are the Western hills and Kunming lake, which experts believe help create a natural flow of qi from the north-west to the south-east.

Afterword

Afterword

The content covered in this modest little book offers only the briefest of glimpses into China's vast cultural legacy. Whole libraries could be dedicated to collecting works on traditional Chinese medicine alone, an area only touched upon here. Thousands of years of a nation's knowledge and achievements are impossible to distil in their entirety, yet we hope that something of the spirit of China and its culture has been conveyed herein.

China has a deep reverence for its culture and traditions, and Chinese people treat those who master aspects of its language and customs with great respect. In China, non-Chinese are known as 'old outsiders' lǎowài 老外, the popular Chinese slang for 'foreigner'), and for such an 'outsider' to attain this knowledge is seen as a special kind of achievement. Such people have historically been labelled as 'old China hands', Zhōngguótōng 中国通, or literally 'China expert'. For centuries, Chinese culture was obscured in a mist of orientalism and mystique, and knowledge about China was highly valued, however scanty or misinformed.

As information about China becomes much more widespread, the age of being lauded as a 'China hand' simply for knowing a few phrases of Mandarin and reeling off the odd anecdote about Qing dynasty history is fast disappearing. Nevertheless, as daunting as it can be, China studies is still a highly rewarding endeavour – even for the casually curious. Armed with a bit of knowledge about China and its culture, the traveller can gain a better understanding of, and get closer to, its warm and welcoming people.

Index

Index